The Customer-Driven Company

Managerial Perspectives on QFD

A number of other titles are available from
the ASI Press, including the following:

**Taguchi Methods and QFD: Hows and Whys for
Management**

Introduction to Quality Engineering

Orthogonal Arrays and Linear Graphs

**Case Studies from the First through Fifth
Symposiums on Taguchi Methods**

**Quality by Design: Taguchi Methods and U.S.
Industry**

**Quality Function Deployment: A Collection of
Presentations and QFD Case Studies**

The Customer-Driven Company

Managerial Perspectives on QFD

William E. Eureka
and
Nancy E. Ryan

ASI Press

Dearborn, Michigan

Published by the ASI Press, a division of the American Supplier
Institute, Inc.

Printed in the United States of America

Library of Congress Cataloging-in-Publication Data

Eureka, William E.
    The customer-driven company : managerial perspectives on
QFD / by William E. Eureka and Nancy E. Ryan.
        p. cm.
    Includes index.
    ISBN 0-941243-03-6
    1. Product management.   2. Quality of products.   I. Ryan,
Nancy E., 1959–   II. Title.
HF5415.15.E95 1988
658.5'62—dc19   88–22174
                                              CIP

Contents

Preface

As the Japanese impact on American industry comes of age, an increasing number of American corporations are aggressively responding to the challenges set forth by their Japanese competitors and striving to produce low-cost products that are "best-in-class," products that clearly meet customer needs. Today, a spirit of renewal and resourcefulness exists that is resulting in a restructuring of industrial America and new, exciting ways of doing business.

Our early understanding of the Japanese advantage caused us to focus on cultural issues that we couldn't reasonably expect to impact and on spectacular results for which there were no known causes. As our understanding of the Japanese advantage matured, however, we learned of operational differences that led to the spectacular results and transcended the cultural issues. An understanding of these operational issues led to the recognition of specific actions, technological tools, and methodologies that could be applied here in America to achieve similar results.

Quality Function Deployment (QFD) is one of these methodologies, and it is especially relevant because it brings out the best in the other technological tools and methodologies. QFD represents the synthesis of numerous methodologies developed in America but perfected and integrated by the Japanese. It is not steeped in theory—rather, it was developed by *users* and is a continually evolving methodology that can be adapted to meet a variety of industrial- and business-related needs.

QFD helps us focus on the details of our business—whether it is manufacturing- or service-oriented—which results in success in the marketplace. It helps us focus our energies on the high-risk details that often go unfulfilled and allows our standard operating system to manage the myriad of lower-risk details. Most importantly, QFD helps us identify and meet customer needs and produce quality- and cost-driven products in an era when not doing so results in slipping market share.

Implementation of QFD in America began in the automotive industry but is rapidly spreading to all major sectors of industry. I have personally witnessed the successful implementation of QFD in both domestic automotive and nonautomotive environments and am looking forward to many more success stories as the benefits of QFD continue to be realized. And I am confident that the creative nature of American managers and engineers will result in innovative applications of QFD that far exceed what the Japanese have accomplished.

This book was written with the above expectations in mind—and in response to the probable questions of newcomers to the methodology. *The Customer-Driven Company: Managerial Perspectives on QFD* will not tell you everything there is to know about QFD. What it *will* tell you is what America's QFD pioneers think and have learned about the methodology; what QFD basically is, involves, and does; and how, where, and when QFD can best be utilized. Hands-on training and application should follow.

William E. Eureka
Vice President and General Manager
American Supplier Institute, Inc.
Dearborn, Michigan
March 31, 1988

Acknowledgments

The ASI Press would like to thank the following people for their contribution to this book:

Michael E. Chupa, Vice President of Marketing, ITT Hancock, Jackson, Michigan.

Dr. Don Clausing, Bernard M. Gordon Adjunct Professor of Engineering Innovation and Practice, Massachusetts Institute of Technology, Cambridge, Massachusetts.

Robert J. Dika, Specialist, Engineering Quality Assurance, Chrysler Corp., Highland Park, Michigan.

Akashi Fukuhara, Assistant Director, Central Japan Quality Control Association, Nagoya, Japan.

James T. Gipprich, Director, Market Development, Kelsey-Hayes Co., Romulus, Michigan.

Calvin W. Gray, Group Vice President, Sales and International Operations, Sheller-Globe, Detroit, Michigan.

Walton M. Hancock, Associate Dean, Center for Research on Integrated Manufacturing, College of Engineering, University of Michigan, Ann Arbor, Michigan.

Norman E. Morrell, Corporate Manager, Quality-Product Reliability, The Budd Co., Troy, Michigan.

George R. Perry, Vice President, Quality and Reliability, Allied-Signal, Inc., Automotive Sector World Headquarters, Southfield, Michigan.

Robert H. Schaefer, Reliability Engineering Director, Product Assurance and Validation, Chevrolet-Pontiac-Canada Group, General Motors Corp., Warren, Michigan.

Raymond P. Smock, Manager, Advanced Quality Concepts Development, Product Assurance, Ford North American Automotive Operations, Dearborn, Michigan.

Peter J. Soltis, Senior Technical Specialist, Product Engineering, Kelsey-Hayes Co., Romulus, Michigan.

Lawrence P. Sullivan, Chairman and Chief Executive Officer, American Supplier Institute, Inc., Dearborn, Michigan.

1

QFD and You

It's time to update the old widget story. Imagine this: Your company has just introduced a new widget—at half the cost and twice the productivity and quality of the competition's widgets, and in two-thirds the time. Contributing to this feat was Quality Function Deployment (QFD)—a system for translating customer requirements into appropriate technical requirements at each stage of the product-development process—and the engineering tools it specifies.

Half the cost and twice the productivity and quality in two-thirds the time—that's what QFD helps achieve, as the following real-life example illustrates. Toyota Motor Corp.'s primary transmission supplier, Aisin Warner, a subsidiary of Aisin Seiki Co., Ltd., Kariya, Japan, used QFD to reduce the number of engineering changes during product development by half. Development time and start-up cycles were also cut in half, enhancing the overall time to market. Numerous other Japanese companies are using QFD to similar avail. They are—or soon will be—your competition.

What exactly is QFD? George R. Perry, Vice President, Quality and Reliability, Allied-Signal, Inc., Southfield, Michigan, defines QFD as "a systematic way of ensuring that the development of product features, characteristics, and specifications, as well as the selection and development of process equipment, methods, and controls, are driven by the demands of the customer or marketplace."

QFD is a system for translating customer requirements into appropriate company requirements at each stage of the product-development cycle, from research and development to engineering, manufacturing, marketing, sales, and distribution (see **Figure 1–1**).

Taken literally, the term Quality Function Deployment may seem a bit misleading. QFD isn't a quality tool—although it can certainly improve quality in the broadest sense of the word. Rather, it's a visually powerful planning tool. And although first used by the Japanese, several aspects of QFD resemble Value Analysis/Value Engineering (VAVE), a process developed in America, combined with marketing techniques.

The term Quality Function Deployment is derived from six Chinese/Japanese characters: *hin shitsu* (qualities, features, or attributes), *ki no* (function), and *ten kai* (deployment, development, or diffusion), as **Figure 1–2** illustrates. The translation is inexact, as well as nondescriptive of the actual QFD process: *Hin shitsu* is synonymous with qualities (i.e., features or attributes), not quality.

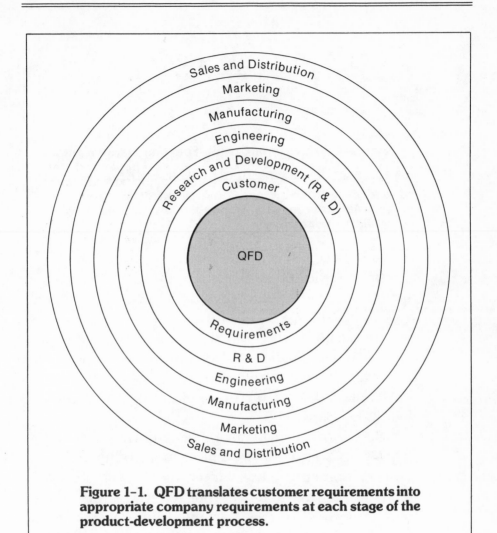

Figure 1-1. QFD translates customer requirements into appropriate company requirements at each stage of the product-development process.

Improved Product Development

QFD brings out the best in a variety of engineering tools already available, which, when properly applied, will help ensure quality products.

With QFD, broad product-development objectives

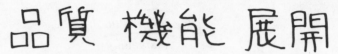

品質　機能　展開

Hin Shitsu   Ki No   Ten Kai
(Quality)   (Function)   (Deployment)

Figure 1-2. The term Quality Function Deployment is derived from six Chinese/Japanese characters: *hin shitsu* (qualities, features, or attributes), *ki no* (function), and *ten kai* (deployment, development, or diffusion). The translation is inexact: *Hin shitsu* is synonymous with qualities, not quality.

are broken down into specific, actionable assignments via a comprehensive team effort. Without this team approach, QFD loses much of its power. The process is accomplished via a series of matrices and charts that deploy customer requirements and related technical requirements from product planning and product design to process planning and the shop floor (see **Figure 1-3**).

On a short-term basis, QFD results in fewer start-up problems, fewer design changes, and shorter product-development cycles—"must haves" for improved engineering productivity and reduced costs. Even more important, however, are such long-term benefits as satisfied customers, lower warranty costs, and increased market share.

When the process is correctly utilized, it creates a closed loop consisting of ever-improving cost, quality, and timeliness; productivity and profitability; and market share. Each of these elements figures prominently in QFD; together, these elements equate to competitive strength—competitive strength that the Japanese are now enjoying (see **Figure 1-4**).

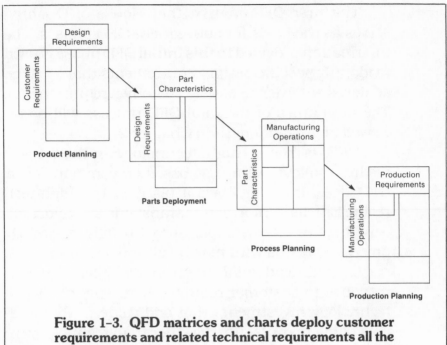

Figure 1-3. QFD matrices and charts deploy customer requirements and related technical requirements all the way down to the shop floor.

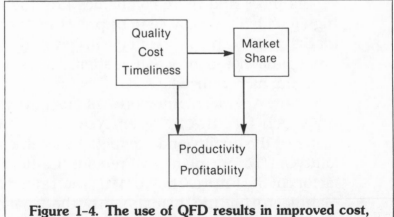

Figure 1-4. The use of QFD results in improved cost, quality, and timeliness, which result in increased productivity and profitability and, ultimately, market share.

The first QFD matrix, the "House of Quality," serves as the basis for subsequent QFD phases. The information provided in this initial QFD phase is used to identify specific design requirements that must be achieved in order to satisfy customer requirements. The mechanics of the total QFD process will be reviewed at greater length in Chapter 2.

QFD is not a high technology; rather, it's a medium-to-low technology based on common sense. QFD does, however, have a place in the high-tech realm: Efficient information transfer is as important, or perhaps even more important, with high-technology processes as it is with more traditional technologies.

QFD can lead to effective technology generation in response to customer requirements. This results in technology investments that add value to the products being manufactured, rather than technology investments that become expensive white elephants. Incremental implementation of new technology can please both coffers and customers.

As more and more companies are finding out, high tech isn't a panacea to be prescribed whenever market share dips, although it can certainly enhance product-development activities after strategic product planning has occurred.

Many American automotive plants have received high-tech facelifts in recent years, yet few have matched the quality and productivity attained at the joint GM/Toyota plant in Fremont, California—no factory of the future. The NUMMI (New United Motors Manufacturing, Inc.) plant is run by the Japanese but employs American workers, discounting the theory that Japanese manufacturing principles won't work in American industrial settings.

"We have to become good at what I call medium

tech," explains Dr. Don Clausing, Bernard M. Gordon Adjunct Professor of Engineering Innovation and Practice at Massachusetts Institute of Technology, Cambridge, Massachusetts. "We tend to want to retrench to high technology because we feel it's where we still have an edge."

Clausing, previously Principal Engineer in the Advanced Development Activities of Xerox Corp., was introduced to QFD in March 1984 while visiting Fuji-Xerox Ltd., Tokyo, Japan. His research into the company's product-development process led to a meeting with one of its primary consultants, Dr. Hajime Makabe. After returning from Japan, Clausing shared his QFD knowledge with engineers from Ford Motor Co., Dearborn, Michigan.

Next came a series of annual American Supplier Institute (ASI), Inc., study missions to Japan that focused increased attention on QFD. QFD has now taken off in the United States—15 years after the methodology was formalized at Kobe Shipyard, Mitsubishi Heavy Industries Ltd., Kobe, Japan.

Kobe Shipyard builds ships that are both massive and sophisticated. Although the shipyard builds only one such ship at a time, the potential benefits of a strategic planning system that details and documents the relationship between the quality of a finished product and that product's components were not lost upon company management.

Is such a system needed in the United States? Yes. By addressing a fundamental weakness of Western society, lack of adequate planning, QFD can help us shore up our weaknesses while building on our strengths. It encourages a comprehensive, holistic approach to product development generally found lacking in American industry.

Quality Defined

The majority of companies doing business in the world today list "produce high-quality products" or "provide high-quality service" as one of their foremost goals. But what, precisely, is a high-quality product or high-quality service? Ask the question more than once and you'll surely get conflicting answers. And do high-quality products always turn a profit? Obviously not. More elementary yet, what exactly *is* quality? To some, it's conformance to specification limits. To others, it's much more.

Quality control, too, is subject to different interpretations. According to *Webster's Ninth New Collegiate Dictionary*, quality control is "an aggregate of activities (as design analysis and statistical sampling with inspection for defects) designed to ensure adequate quality, especially in manufactured products."

Another standard reference source, the *McGraw-Hill Dictionary of Scientific and Technical Terms*, prefers this definition: "inspection, analysis, and action applied to a portion of the product in a manufacturing operation to estimate overall quality of the product and determine what, if any, changes must be made to achieve or maintain the required level of quality."

"Glossary and Tables for Statistical Quality Control," published by the American Society for Quality Control, on the other hand, defines quality control as "the overall system of activities whose purpose is to provide a quality of product or service that meets the needs of users; also, the use of such a system."

The Japanese definition of quality control differs even more markedly. As recorded in Japan Industrial Standard Z8101–1981, "Quality control is a system of means to economically produce goods or services that satisfy customer requirements. Implementing quality control effectively necessitates the cooperation of all people in the company, involving top management, managers, supervisors, and workers in all areas of corporate activities, such as market research, research and development, product planning, design, preparations for production, purchasing, vendor management, manufacturing, inspection, sales and after services, as well as financial control, personnel administration, and training and education. Quality control carried out in this manner is called Company-Wide Quality Control."

In addition, the Japanese concept of quality appears to be more comprehensive than the characteristics usually associated with quality, encompassing performance, extra features (added options), reliability, durability, serviceability, aesthetics, and conformance to standards.

Like beauty, quality is in the eye of the beholder. The beholder, in the case of product-development activities, should be the customer. Hence, any definition of quality should be supplied by the customer—which is what QFD ensures. Quality, which is in the eye of the customer, is communicated via the "voice of the customer."

The Need for QFD

As consumers become more cost- and value-conscious, they're turning to alternative sources for products. Lucrative price incentives may temporarily appease these consumers and increase market share, but they aren't a viable long-term business approach.

As competitors match price incentives, the net result is to lower the profit margin of the respective industrial sector.

These value-conscious consumers are demanding ever-improving levels of quality. When they don't get it, they go elsewhere. And a customer lost because of a quality problem may never return—and may take 20 or more other customers with him or her.

Time to market is increasingly critical for capturing market share: It's easier to capture market share by being first to market with a desirable product than to win customers back with a late entry. Companies with lengthy product-development cycles are especially vulnerable: Such product-development cycles make it extremely difficult to forecast market requirements. Reduced product-development cycles help companies more accurately match products to consumers and take the guesswork out of market forecasting.

Quality, cost, timeliness, and productivity are often viewed as conflicting elements that require the making of trade-offs. The best Japanese companies, however, have learned to successfully optimize these apparently conflicting objectives while making minimal trade-offs, achieving both increased market share and profits and loyal customer followings.

QFD has played an important part in this optimization, helping improve quality, timeliness, and productivity while reducing costs.

Focus: Problem Prevention

The best Japanese companies deploy the voice of the customer to help determine important product attributes. Engineers at these Japanese companies then design and build to target values, seeking to reduce manufacturing variation around these targets. The Japanese focus on optimizing the product and the process, not only to maximize performance but also to reduce variation. This results in consistent high performance, from product to product and throughout the product's lifetime.

By front-loading product-development efforts, the Japanese focus on planning and problem prevention, not problem solving. QFD is one of the methodologies used to make the transition from reactive to preventive—from downstream, manufacturing-oriented quality control to upstream, product-design-oriented quality control (see **Figure 1–5**). It does so by defining "what to do" and "how to do it" in a manner that results in the consistent performance that satisfies customers.

By clearly defining the job objectives needed to achieve it, QFD helps build customer-defined quality into a product. While it doesn't *guarantee* success,

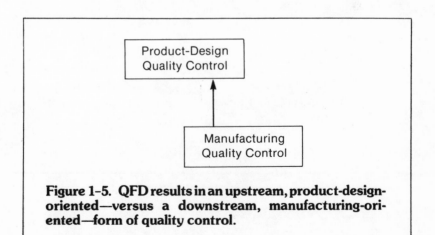

Figure 1-5. QFD results in an upstream, product-design-oriented—versus a downstream, manufacturing-oriented—form of quality control.

QFD greatly improves the probability of achieving it. Without QFD, you get what you've always gotten. With it, you get a new, improved approach to product planning.

2

The QFD Approach

"Back when a knight went to a specialized blacksmith to have a coat of armor constructed, things were much simpler—the customer was speaking directly to the blacksmith, who could then do Quality Function Deployment (QFD) in his head," explains MIT's Don Clausing. But in today's complex industrial environment, the customer and the shop-floor operators manufacturing his or her product seldom speak to each other. QFD brings the *voice of the customer* directly to the shop floor.

QFD deploys the voice of the customer—*customer requirements* defined by detailed consultation, brainstorming, feedback mechanisms, and market research—through the total product-development process. This involves translating customer requirements into appropriate technical requirements for each stage of product development and production (see **Figure 2–1**).

Developing a top-notch project team is one of the

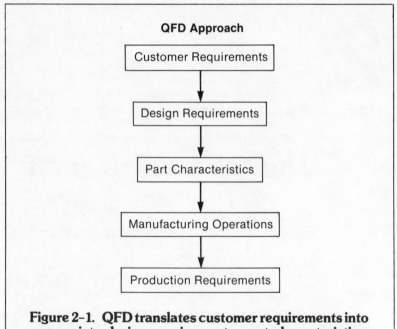

QFD Approach

Customer Requirements

Design Requirements

Part Characteristics

Manufacturing Operations

Production Requirements

Figure 2-1. QFD translates customer requirements into appropriate design requirements, part characteristics, manufacturing operations, and production requirements.

most challenging—and potentially rewarding—aspects of the process. All areas involved in product development should be represented on this team: marketing, product planning, product design and engineering, prototyping and testing, process development, manufacturing, assembly, sales, and service. All should be working toward a shared goal: a customer-defined product to be completed by a specific date and at a specific cost.

Laying the Foundation

The basic approach used in QFD is conceptually similar to the practice followed by most American manufacturing companies. The process begins with customer requirements, which are usually loosely stated qualitative characteristics, such as "looks good," "easy to use," "works well," "feels good," "safe," "comfortable," "lasts long," "luxurious," etc. These characteristics are important to the customer but often defy quantification and are difficult to act on.

During product development, customer requirements are converted into internal company requirements called *design requirements.* These requirements are generally global product characteristics (usually measurable) that will satisfy customer requirements if properly executed.

Product development does not usually begin at this global level, however; rather, it begins at the system, subsystem, or parts level. Global design requirements are hence translated into critical *part characteristics* that allow the essential functions of the product to be performed.

The use of the word *parts* here and in the following sections is appropriate for products that are assemblies of mechanical components. QFD applies equally well to other types of products; for example, combinations of ingredients, materials, or services. "Ingredients," "materials," "services," or other relevant terminology may be substituted for "parts" in this and subsequent discussions.

Determining the required *manufacturing operations* is the next step, a step that's often constrained by previous capital investments of factories and equipment. Within these operating constraints, the manufacturing operations most critical to creating the desired part characteristics are determined, as are the process parameters of the most influential operations.

The manufacturing operations are then translated into the *production requirements* shop-floor personnel will use to consistently produce the required part characteristics. These include inspection and Statistical Process Control (SPC) plans, preventive-maintenance programs, and operator instructions and training, as well as mistake-proofing devices for preventing inadvertent operator errors—the entire set of procedures and practices that aid in the manufacture of products that will ultimately satisfy customer requirements.

This hierarchical approach is not unlike the approach American companies have used for years with varying degrees of success. But problems occur when some of the translations are not properly made. There are several key reasons for these improper translations, including large organizational structures and complex product-development processes.

American companies are normally structured with strong vertical line organizations with fairly clear reporting hierarchies. When a new program of great importance is to be implemented, the lines of many departments must be spanned, forming the horizontal linkages necessary to complete the program. The vertical linkages, however, are often so strong that departmental loyalties are at odds with program requirements.

The Japanese compare strong vertical and horizontal linkages to a well-constructed piece of fabric—for a good weave, both the vertical and the horizontal threads must be strong (see **Figure 2–2**). Although the Japanese also have line organizations, cross-functional activities are strengthened through the use of QFD.

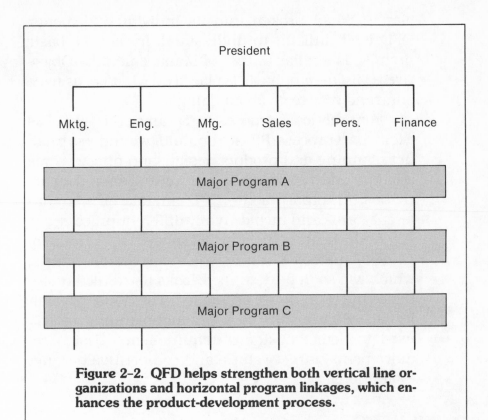

Figure 2–2. QFD helps strengthen both vertical line organizations and horizontal program linkages, which enhances the product-development process.

Before QFD can begin, however, who the customer is must be determined. In most instances, more than one customer exists—e.g., the end user, the company the product is being produced for, and the assembly operator who will be putting the product together. In almost all cases, there will be both external and internal customers. Both need to be taken into account—but should a conflict arise, the internal should almost always take a back seat to the external, ensuring that the end users get what they want.

QFD is accomplished through a series of charts and matrices that may seem very complex at first glance. When broken into its individual elements, QFD isn't difficult to understand. In fact, its basic premise is similar to that of Management by Objectives (MBO)—emphasis is placed on what needs to be done and how to go about doing it.

For practical purposes, QFD can be thought of as a four-part process: Phases one and two address product planning and product design, and phases three and four address process planning and shop-floor activities. (In actual practice, QFD may take on many different forms and include many different processes.)

At the heart of the first QFD phase is the *House of Quality* matrix. (This matrix's correlation matrix, which will soon be described, looks like a tiled roof—hence the term House of Quality.) The House of Quality (see **Figure 2–3**) is a product-planning matrix used to depict customer requirements, design requirements, target values, and competitive product evaluations.

Building a House of Quality

The following summary of House of Quality components will help clarify the content and function of each: Touring the rooms of the House of Quality will help us understand the house itself. But first, let's examine a recurring QFD theme: from "what" to "how" to "how much" (see **Figure 2–4**).

This theme is based on an input-output strategy. QFD begins with a list of loosely stated objectives—the "whats" we want to accomplish. These "what" items are the basic customer requirements. They will probably be vague and require further detailed definition. One such "what" item might be an excellent cup of

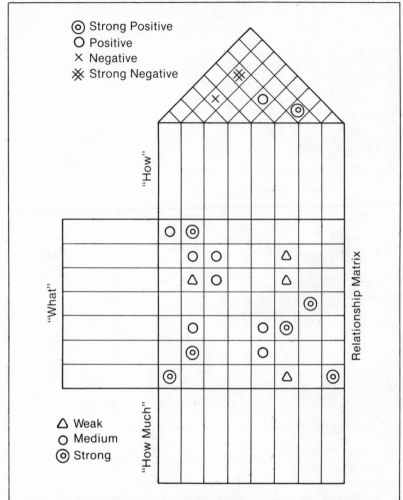

Figure 2-3. The House of Quality product-planning matrix charts customer requirements, design requirements, target values, and competitive-product evaluations.

coffee (see **Figure 2-5**). Every coffee drinker wants this, but providing it requires further definition.

To provide the required further definition, each "what" item is broken into one or more "how" items.

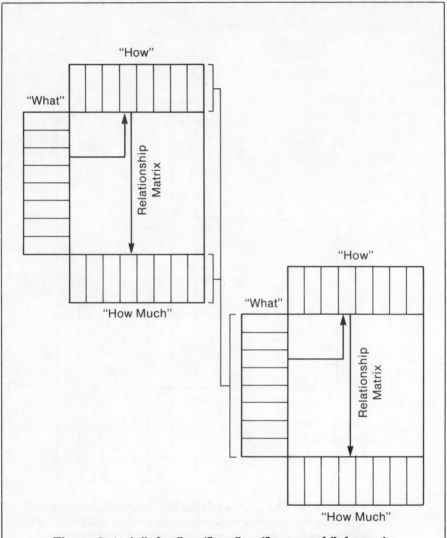

Figure 2-4. A "what" to "how" to "how much" theme is common to most QFD matrices and charts. This theme is based on an input-output strategy: "What" items are broken into "how" items, and then the "how" items evolve into new "what" items.

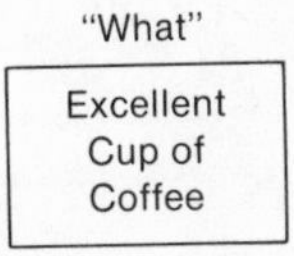

"What"

| Excellent |
| Cup of |
| Coffee |

Figure 2–5. "What" items are the basic customer require-ments—in this example, an excellent cup of coffee.

This process is similar to the process of refining marketing specifications into system-level engineering specifications. Customer requirements are actually being translated into design requirements. The excellent cup of coffee requirement, for example, would be translated into "hot," "eye-opener," "rich flavor," "good aroma," "low price," "generous amount," and "stays hot" (see **Figure 2–6**). (If the cup of coffee were being served in a restaurant, "service with a smile" and "free refills" might also be customer requirements or "how" items. Customer requirements and conditions of use are correlated.)

"How" items also usually require further definition—and are thus treated as new "what" items that are broken into additional "how" items. This is similar to the process of translating system-level specifications into parts-level specifications. With the cup of coffee example, new "how" items might be "serving temperature," "amount of caffeine," "flavor component," "flavor intensity," "aroma component," "aroma intensity," "sale price," "volume," and "temperature after serving" (see **Figure 2–7**).

This refinement process is continued until every item on the list is actionable. Such detail is necessary because there's no way of ensuring successful realiza-

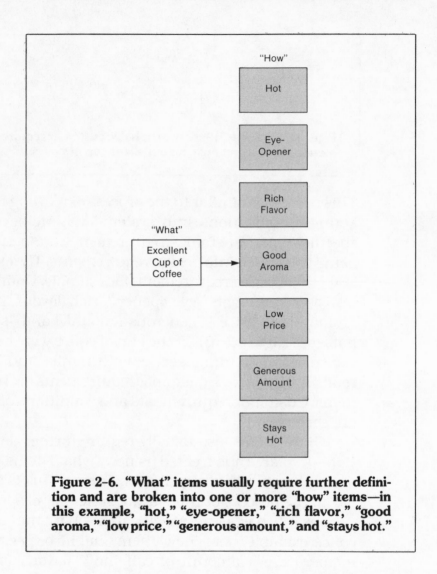

**Figure 2-6. "What" items usually require further defini-
tion and are broken into one or more "how" items—in
this example, "hot," "eye-opener," "rich flavor," "good
aroma," "low price," "generous amount," and "stays hot."**

tion of a requirement that no one knows how to
accomplish!

Unfortunately, this process is complicated by the
fact that some of the "how" items affect more than one
"what" item—and can even affect one another. Only
about half of all product-improvement efforts are

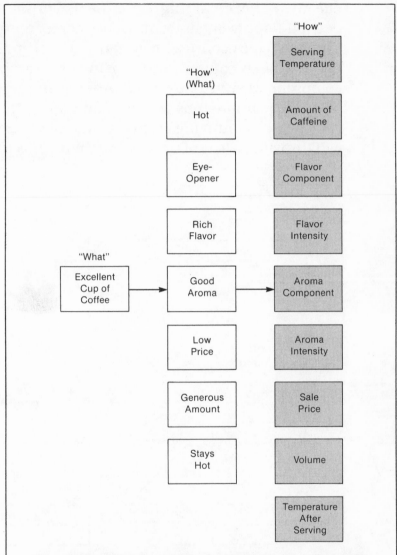

Figure 2-7. "How" items also usually require further definition and are treated as new "what" items. These are then broken into additional "how" items—in this example, "serving temperature," "amount of caffeine," "flavor component," "flavor intensity," "aroma component," "aroma intensity," "sale price," "volume," and "temperature after serving."

effective—the remaining 50% either fail to provide the desired improvement or introduce some unexpected problem. This occurs with even the best of engineers, because such complex relationships cannot be fully comprehended in one's head. Attempting to clearly trace the relationships of "what" and "how" items becomes quite confusing at this point (see **Figure 2–8**). QFD provides a way of untangling this complex web of

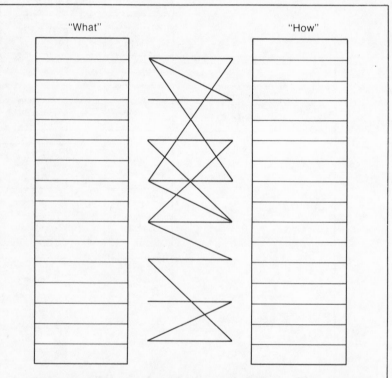

Figure 2–8. Clearly tracing the relationships of "what" and "how" items can be confusing—some "how" items affect more than one "what" item and can even affect one another. The House of Quality matrix simplifies this process.

relationships via a matrix bordered by "how" and "what" items that defines the relationships.

The customer-defined "what" items are listed to the left of the relationship matrix on a vertical axis. The "how" items (design requirements) are listed on a horizontal axis above the relationship matrix (see **Figure 2–9**).

Next, the relationships of the "what" and "how" items are symbolically represented: Unique symbols

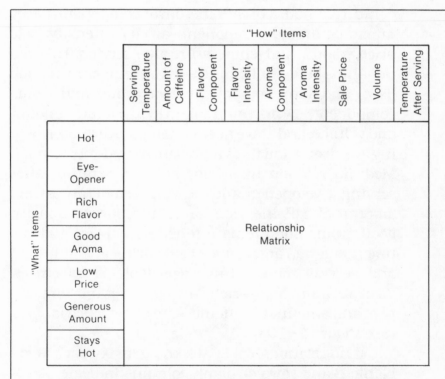

Figure 2–9. The "what" items are listed to the left of the House of Quality's relationship matrix on a vertical axis. The "how" items are listed on a horizontal axis above the relationship matrix.

are used to depict weak, medium, and strong relationships between customer requirements and design requirements. Commonly used symbols are a triangle for weak relationships, a circle for medium relationships, and a double circle for strong relationships.

For example, customer requirements ("what" items) identified for an excellent cup of coffee were hot, eye-opener, rich flavor, good aroma, low price, generous amount, and stays hot. Corresponding design requirements ("how" items) were serving temperature, amount of caffeine, flavor component, flavor intensity, aroma component, aroma intensity, sale price, volume, and temperature after serving. The relationships between hot and serving temperature, rich flavor and flavor component, good aroma and aroma component, low price and sale price, generous amount and volume, and stays hot and temperature after serving are strong and thus represented by double circles. Medium relationships—hot and temperature after serving, eye-opener and serving temperature and amount of caffeine, rich flavor and flavor intensity, good aroma and aroma intensity, low price and volume, generous amount and sale price, and stays hot and serving temperature—are depicted by circles. Weak relationships—rich flavor and serving temperature and amount of caffeine—are shown as triangles. (See **Figure 2–10**.)

If no relationship exists, the matrix space is left blank. Blank rows or blank columns indicate places where the translation of "what" items into "how" items is inadequate, providing an opportunity for valuable cross-checking. The QFD process provides numerous opportunities for cross-checking, which is

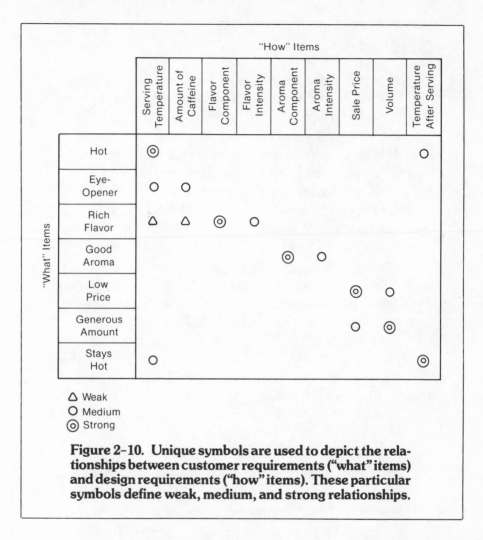

Figure 2-10. Unique symbols are used to depict the relationships between customer requirements ("what" items) and design requirements ("how" items). These particular symbols define weak, medium, and strong relationships.

one of its greatest strengths. The ability of QFD to evolve plans into actions while repeatedly cross-checking one's thinking also makes it useful for any non-trivial planning function, including business plans and internal business systems (see sidebar, "QFD for Strategic Planning," p. 44).

Running parallel with the "how" axis on the bot-

Success in the U.S.

The result of the first Quality Function Deployment (QFD) case study performed at Kelsey-Hayes Co., Romulus, Michigan, was a customer-driven design for a new electromechanical product—a coolant-level sensor. The study was performed in conjunction with the American Supplier Institute, Inc., and Ford Motor Co., for which the sensor was being produced.

The QFD study was composed of three parts: Phase I, assembly and component features; Phase II, material and design; and Phase III, manufacturing processes. The market-quality (customer) requirements were broken into functional and performance requirements. Functional requirements were then broken into customer and operation categories; performance requirements were broken into serviceability and durability.

After completion of an initial House of Quality for the coolant-level sensor, the housing was identified as the most critical product (design) requirement. A House of

tom edge of the relationship matrix is a third element, the "how much" axis. "How much" items are measurements for the "how" items. They're kept separate from the "how" items because when the "hows" are determined, the values of the "how much" items usually aren't known. These values will be determined through analysis.

"How much" items provide both an objective means of ensuring that requirements have been met and targets for further detailed development. Thus, they provide specific objectives that guide the subsequent design and afford a means of objectively assess-

Quality was then completed for the housing itself. Key customer functional and performance requirements included "easy-to-add coolant," "easy-to-identify unit," and "provide cap-removal instructions."

As a result of the QFD study, a coolant-level sensor was designed with product features that would best meet the above functional and performance requirements. Included in the final production design, for example, were slotted holes in the tube to allow coolant to freely flow to the coolant reservoir. Also, the words "radiator coolant only" in raised yellow lettering and a single tab labeled "lift" were added to the housing cap.

The QFD study was beneficial in more ways than one. "As an engineer on that first project, I'm able to say that doing a QFD study made me aware of the product in terms of how it would fulfill customer requirements," explains Peter J. Soltis, Senior Technical Specialist, Product Engineering, at Kelsey-Hayes.

ing progress. Whenever possible, "how much" items should be measurable. Measurable entities tend to be more actionable—they provide more opportunity for analysis and optimization than nonmeasurable entities. Without measurements to work toward, the goal is often merely to "do better." On the other hand, "what gets measured gets improved." If most of the "how much" items aren't measurable, "how" item definitions probably aren't detailed enough.

"How much" items for the cup of coffee example include 120–140 °F, —— ppm, less than $.25, greater than 12 fl. oz., and 110–125 °F (see **Figure 2-11**).

"How" Items

"What" Items	Serving Temperature	Amount of Caffeine	Flavor Component	Flavor Intensity	Aroma Component	Aroma Intensity	Sale Price	Volume	Temperature After Serving
Hot	◎								
Eye-Opener	○	○							
Rich Flavor	△	△	◎	○					
Good Aroma					◎	○			
Low Price							◎	○	
Generous Amount							○	◎	
Stays Hot	○								◎
"How Much" Items	120-140 °F	—— ppm	Established by Judges	Established by Judges	Established by Judges	Established by Judges	Less Than $.25	Greater Than 12 Fl. Oz.	110-125 °F

△ Weak
○ Medium
◎ Strong

Figure 2-11. "How much" items (e.g., 120-140 °F, —— ppm, less than $.25, greater than 12 fl. oz., and 110-125 °F), measurements for the "how" items, are listed at the bottom edge of the House of Quality's relationship matrix on a horizontal axis.

"How much" items related to the flavor and aroma customer requirements are determined by a panel of judges.

The what/how/how much process forms the basis for almost all QFD charts—it's the key that unlocks the House of Quality. Enhancing this process are the following: correlation matrix, competitive assessment, and rating and weighting.

Correlation Matrix

The triangular *correlation matrix* (the "roof" of the House of Quality and the source of its name) is located parallel to and above the "how" axis (see **Figure 2-12**). This matrix describes the correlation between each "how" item via unique symbols that represent positive or negative ratings and the strength of each relationship (i.e., positive, negative, strong positive, or strong negative correlation). Commonly used symbols are a circle (positive), double circle (strong positive), cross (negative), and double cross (strong negative). By charting conflicting relationships (negatives and strong negatives), the matrix facilitates timely resolution of trade-off issues.

The correlation matrix can be used to identify which "how" items support one another and which are in conflict. The assignment of positive or negative ratings is based on each "how" item's influence in achieving other "how" items, regardless of the direction in which the "how much" value moves. In positive correlations, one "how" item supports another "how" item. In negative correlations, the two "how" items are in conflict.

Both positive and negative correlations provide important information. Positive correlations help

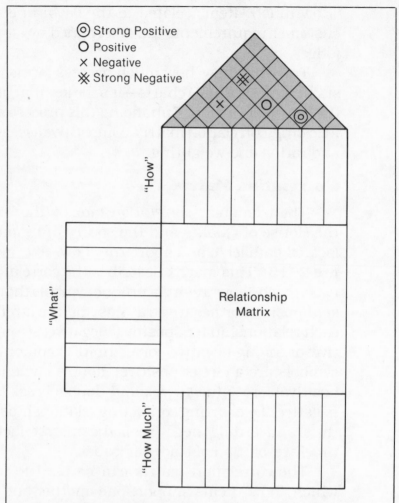

Figure 2–12. The correlation matrix, which describes the correlation between each "how" item via unique symbols that represent positive or negative ratings and the strength of each relationship, is located parallel to and above the "how" axis.

identify "how" items that are closely related and avoid duplication of effort across company lines. Negative correlations represent conditions that will probably require trade-offs—conditions that should never be avoided. Trade-offs that aren't identified and resolved lead to unfulfilled customer requirements. Trade-offs are resolved by adjusting the "how much" values.

Competitive Assessment

Two *competitive-assessment graphs* (see **Figure 2-13**) provide an item-by-item comparison between a company's product and similar competitive products. The first of these graphs (listed on a vertical axis to the right of the relationship matrix) corresponds to the "what" items and the second (listed on a horizontal axis to the right of the relationship matrix) corresponds to the "how" items.

Competitive assessment of the "what" items is also called *customer competitive assessment* and should use customer-oriented information; *technical competitive assessment*, which should use engineering-generated information, is another name for competitive assessment of the "how" items.

The competitive-assessment graphs can be used to establish competitive "how much" values and help position a product in the marketplace. They're also extremely beneficial when used to detect gaps or errors in engineering judgment—including instances where in-house evaluations don't coincide with the voice of the customer. If the "how" items have properly evolved

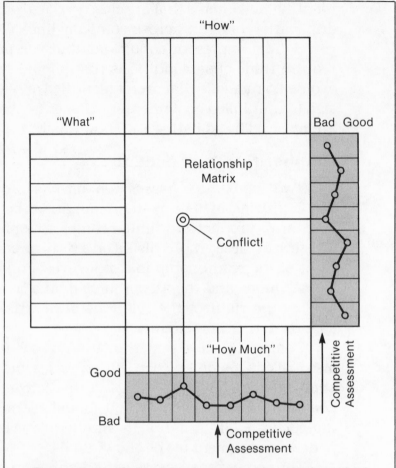

Figure 2–13. Competitive-assessment graphs, which provide an item-by-item comparison between a company's product and similar competitive products, are listed on a vertical axis to the right of the House of Quality's relationship matrix and on a horizontal axis below the relationship matrix.

from the "what" items, their competitive assessments should be similar. Strongly related "what" and "how" items should also exhibit a similar competitive-assessment relationship.

Rating and Weighting

Charts or graphs that numerically *rate and weight* the "what" and "how" items in terms of the desired end result are also useful. Rating of the "what" items is performed on a one-to-five scale. A numerical rating of one-to-five is placed in a column to the immediate right of each "what" item to reflect the relative importance of this item to the customer. These ratings are then multiplied by the weights assigned to each matrix symbol (weak, medium, and strong).

The standard 9-3-1 weighting system is often used, although alternative systems can be applied to the same effect, placing stronger emphasis on the most important items. The results of the rating and weighting exercises are then recorded on a horizontal axis below the "how much" items (see **Figure 2-14**). This results in the identification of critical product requirements (which translate to critical customer requirements) and aids in the trade-off decision-making process.

The above example of a House of Quality is just that—an example. Houses of Quality can be built in many shapes and forms to meet almost any need—what's important is that they be tailored to the application. Some of the additional elements that can be included are key selling points, the level of technical difficulty, technical standards, and quality standards.

Subsequent QFD Phases

Building a House of Quality is the first—and most frequently applied—phase of the QFD procedure. The next phase deploys some of the design requirements

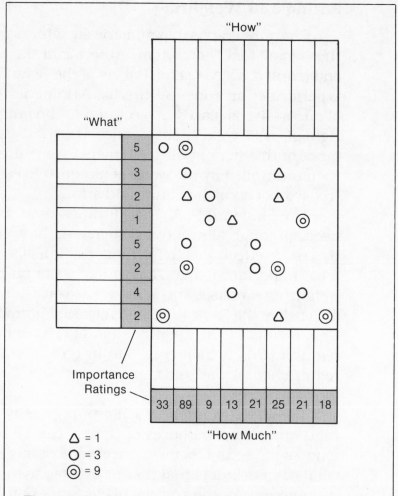

Figure 2–14. **Charts or graphs that numerically rate and weight the "what" and "how" items are located to the right of the vertical "what" axis and below the horizontal "how much" axis.**

identified in the House of Quality phase to the subsystem/parts level. The resulting parts-deployment matrix serves as the basis for all preliminary design activities. It's important to note, however, that not all of the

House of Quality design requirements need to be deployed. Rather, only the high-risk (new, difficult, or extremely important) design requirements are carried forth. This ensures that time and effort aren't wasted on design requirements that are already being successfully achieved.

This matrix physically resembles the House of Quality matrix. Customer requirements and design requirements are described in precise engineering terms in this matrix, and competitive evaluations and target values are further developed.

The *parts-deployment* phase (**Figure 2–15**) utilizes such supporting activities as Value Analysis/

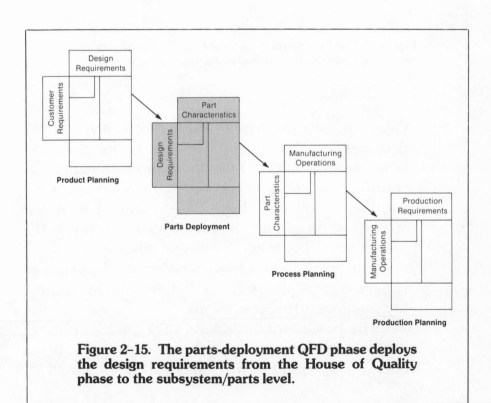

Figure 2–15. The parts-deployment QFD phase deploys the design requirements from the House of Quality phase to the subsystem/parts level.

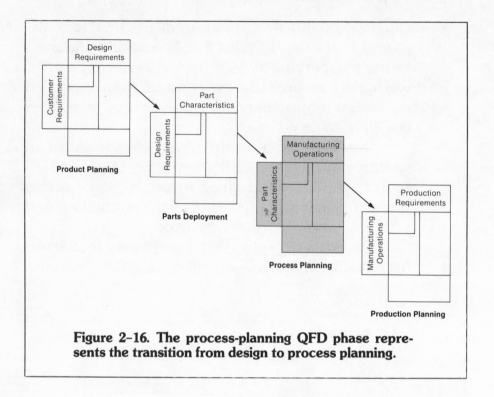

Figure 2–16. The process-planning QFD phase represents the transition from design to process planning.

Value Engineering (VAVE), Fault-Tree Analysis (FTA), Reverse Fault-Tree Analysis (RFTA), Failure-Mode and Effect Analysis (FMEA), design optimization, process optimization, cost analysis, and parts selection for reliability assurance. This phase culminates in the identification of part characteristics critical to the execution of the design requirements.

The critical part characteristics are highlighted in a parts-deployment chart that, in turn, helps identify manufacturing operations.

The *process-planning* phase (**Figure 2–16**) represents the transition from design to manufacturing operations. A process-planning chart is prepared for each critical part characteristic at this phase.

The following information is included in each process-planning chart: a listing of the required processes, a matrix graphing the relationship between each process and each critical part characteristic, and listings of process-control parameters.

This information is used to produce process-control charts for each part. During this phase, a process FMEA is conducted, and the information from the previous charts is verified and reviewed.

The *production-planning* phase (**Figure 2–17**) transfers the information generated in the subse-

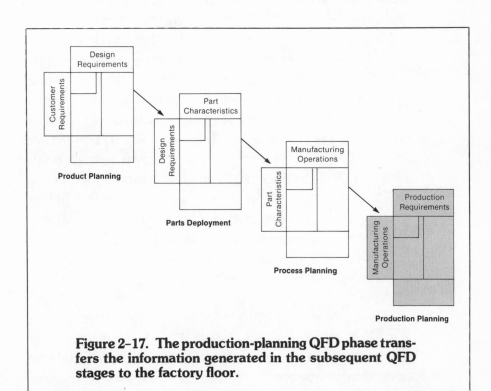

Figure 2–17. The production-planning QFD phase transfers the information generated in the subsequent QFD stages to the factory floor.

quent phases to the factory floor. A series of tables and charts is used to accomplish this.

This phase deploys information relevant to a number of functions. Like the other QFD phases, it can be adapted to meet a wide variety of requirements. QFD thrives on flexibility.

Focus: Flexibility

According to Akashi Fukuhara, Assistant Director, Central Japan Quality Control Association (CJQCA), Nagoya, Japan, "QFD is not only found in manufacturing in Japan—it's also used in the service industry, the construction industry, the computer-software industry, as well as other industries."

QFD can be used in applications apart from product development, such as improvement of existing processes and internal-system evaluations.

The Budd Co., Troy, Michigan, was one of the first companies to initiate a QFD case study in the United States. The groundwork for this study was laid in late 1985. By April 1986, Budd had developed two partial QFD case studies. QFD is part of a total quality-management program aimed at continuous planned quality improvement under way at Budd. The process addresses what Budd's senior management team has coined "survival issues for the 1990s": product quality and cost.

Budd's initial efforts were critiqued by Toyota supplier engineers and one of QFD's founding fathers, Dr. Shigeru Mizuno, during ASI's fifth annual Japanese study mission.

"Going to Japan and having our case studies critiqued was a good learning experience for us," explains Norman E. Morrell, Corporate Manager, Quality-Product Reliability, at Budd. "When we came back, we felt that we understood the application for new products, but we still believed there was a great deal to be done with existing processes. So our Stamping and Frame Division explored using QFD for improving its engineering proposal system. We've also had success with that type of application."

The application of the QFD process to Budd's engineering proposal system began with a definition of customer (in this case internal-user) requirements. This was accomplished via interviews with users from each department affected by the system: sales, product engineering, manufacturing engineering, industrial engineering, plant engineering, purchasing, estimating, and quality.

Three basic customer requirements ("what" items) were then identified: communication, information, and response time. These "what" items were placed on a vertical axis to the left of the relationship matrix (see **Figure 2–18**).

Two subsequent levels of detail were then identified. Communication, for example, was broken into weekly meetings, assumptions, distribution, and tracking system. These items were then refined even further; i.e., progress update, product ground rules, more feedback, and priority system were extracted from weekly meetings. These finer details are shown in **Figure 2–18** as second- and third-level requirements. The second- and third-level items were listed to the right of the basic customer requirements on a vertical axis.

Engineering proposal features were then defined by determining the various responsibilities of all de-

(5) A – STRONG CORRELATION
(3) B – MEDIUM CORRELATION
(1) C – SMALL CORRELATION

ENGINEERING PROPOSAL SYSTEM

ENGINEERING PROPOSAL FEATURES

USER REQUIREMENTS

Primary	Secondary	Tertiary	RATING	CUSTOMER REQUEST	RESPONSE TIME	SUMMARY SHEET	PART INFORMATION	CUSTOMER CONTACT	DIE PROCESS	ASSEMBLY PROCESS	TIMING	MANPOWER	CAPITAL EQUIPMENT	FEASIBILITY	PROTOTYPE COST	PURCHASED PARTS	LABOR COST	MATERIAL COST	TOOLING COST	PIECE PRICE	DISTRIBUTION	PURCHASED TOOLING	EVALUATION POINTS
COMMUNICATION	WEEKLY MEETINGS (5)	PROGRESS UPDATE	3	C/3																			15
		PRODUCT GROUND RULES	5	C/5	A/25	A/25	C/5	B/15	B/15	B/15			B/15				B/15	B/15	B/15	B/15			900
		MORE FEEDBACK	1	A/5	B/3								C/1							C/1			30
		PRIORITY SYSTEM	4	B/12	A/20	B/12							B/12							C/4			240
	ASSUMPTIONS (3)	WHAT ARE THE ASSUMPTIONS	3	C/3	A/15		B/9	A/15	A/15		C/3												180
		ALL WORKING TO SAME ASSUMPTIONS	3	C/3	A/15			A/15	A/15		C/3												153
	DISTRIBUTION (2)	RECEIVE SUMMARY SHEET SOONER	4	B/12	C/4									B/12	B/12	B/12	B/12	B/12	A/20				168
		COST DATA REQUEST FROM PROD. ENG.	2	A/10									A/10				C/2						44
		REQUEST FOR INFO. FROM PROC. ENG.	2	A/10													C/2			A/10			44
	TRACKING SYSTEM (3)	WHICH PLANT HAS "E.P."	2	C/2																C/2			12
		STATUS REPORT	3	C/3																			9
INFORMATION	SUMMARY SHEET (5)	PRODUCTION REQUIREMENTS	5	A/25	C/5	C/5		B/15	B/15	A/25	C/5		A/25			C/5	C/5	C/5	C/5		C/5		925
		PART MODELS & YR.	5	A/25		A/25	A/25					B/15	C/5			B/15	A/25		B/15				950
		COMPLETE LIST OF PARTS	5	A/25	C/5	A/25	C/5	A/25	A/25	A/25	C/5	C/5	C/5	A/25	C/5	C/5	C/5	C/5	C/5				1150
		DELIVERY DESTINATION	4	A/20	C/4	A/20						B/12	C/4			B/12	B/12		A/20		C/4		980
		PART SPECIFICATIONS	4	A/20	C/4	A/20	A/20	C/4	A/20	A/20			B/12	C/4			A/20	B/12		C/4			840
		MATERIAL SPECS	3		A/15	A/15		B/9	B/9								A/15						315
		PLANTS AFFECTED	5	A/25						A/25	A/25		A/25				A/25			C/5			525
	PROCESS (5)	INCLUDE COMPLETE PART INFO.	3	C/3		A/15	A/15	A/15	A/15	C/3	A/15		C/3			B/9		A/15		C/3			480
		COMPLETE CLARIFICATION OF PROCESS OPERATIONS	4	C/4		A/20	A/20	A/20	C/4	C/4			A/20			A/20	A/20		C/4				700
	PART INFORMATION (5)	ASSEMBLY BREAK-DOWN	4		A/20	B/12	C/4	A/20	A/20	C/4	C/4		C/4	B/12		A/20	C/4	A/20	C/4			780
		DRAWINGS	5	A/25	B/15	A/25	C/5	A/25	A/25	C/5			A/25			C/5	A/25		B/15	B/15		1100
		ALL WORKING TO SAME INFO.	3	A/15	C/3		C/3	B/9	B/9	C/3	C/3	A/15	C/3			C/3	A/15	A/15				345
		ALL WORKING TO SAME PART LEVEL	3	A/15			C/3	B/9	A/15	A/15	C/3	C/3	B/9			C/3	C/3	A/15	A/15			600
RESPONSE	BETTER INFORMATION (3)	MORE COMPLETE SUMMARY SHEET	4	C/4	A/20	A/20	B/12		A/20	A/20	C/4	C/4	C/4			C/4	C/4	C/4	C/4			372
		PARTS RECEIVED BY COMPUTER GRAPHICS	1	C/1		A/5		C/1	C/1													24
	QUICKER RESPONSE (5)	BETTER RESPONSE ON ADDITIONAL INFO. REQUEST	3	A/15		C/3	A/15	A/15	A/15													315
		STREAMLINE PAPER WORK	2	A/10	A/10															A/10		150
		STANDARDIZE PROCESS FORMAT	2	C/2			A/10	A/10		C/2												120
	OPERATING INSTRUCTION (3)	SET OF RULES	3	A/15	C/3	C/3						A/15	A/15						A/15	A/15		243
		CONTINUITY	3	A/15	C/3	C/3						A/15	C/3						A/15	C/3		171
		FORMALIZE PROCEDURE	3	A/15									C/3						A/15	C/3		108
		EVALUATION POINTS		136	275	313	143	66	289	289	124	51	89	16	62	70	100	131	125	219	97	51	

Figure 2–18. The Budd Co., Troy, Michigan, has applied QFD to its engineering proposal system.

partments involved. These "how" items included such elements as customer request, part information, capital equipment, purchased parts, tooling cost, and distribution. The engineering proposal features were listed on a horizontal axis at the relationship matrix's upper edge, perpendicular to the customer requirements.

Each customer requirement and engineering-proposal-feature correlation was then weighted and rated, which resulted in a system-wide evaluation for the engineering-proposal procedure.

Budd's Stamping and Frame Division has applied QFD to improve die-change times and for tool design and construction. In these instances, the customer is the Budd plant that will be using the process or product in question. Budd's Wheel and Brake Division is using QFD for more traditional product-development applications.

The Budd Co.'s commitment to continuous planned quality improvement has naturally led to a study that addresses customer wants in the broadest possible application of QFD. Management representing all functions across divisional and product lines is meeting to address the issue of satisfying the customer's need for reduced time and improved effectiveness in new vehicle introduction. An integral question, "Are we satisfying the customer?," is posed on a regular basis. In Morrell's mind, customer satisfaction is the key to a company's future. And QFD helps to achieve it.

QFD for Strategic Planning

Quality Function Deployment (QFD) can be used in both the plant and corporate offices. Although typically thought of as a product-development tool, it can also be applied to strategic planning in industrial and nonindustrial environments. **Figure S2–1** provides a framework for how QFD can be used in strategic planning.

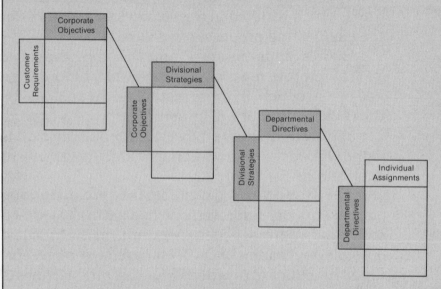

Figure S2–1.

Example 1 and Example 2 show how QFD can be applied in two different business environments. For simplicity's sake, a two-phase QFD procedure has been used in each example.

EXAMPLE 1

A machine-tool manufacturer identified the following objectives ("what" items), which were broken into more actionable goals ("how" items that will become new "what" items) and strategies ("how" items for the goals).

Objectives

- Improved product quality and reliability
- Reduced delivery times and costs for new products

Goals

- Reduce number of monthly downtime incidents (mean time between failures)
- Introduce enhanced flexible manufacturing systems
- Reduce delivery time for special orders
- Obtain cost savings on upgrades of existing products

Strategies

- Implement simultaneous engineering partnerships with suppliers
- Apply Taguchi Methods (see appendix, p. 103) and QFD at the design stage
- Institute preventive-maintenance training for customers

The above objectives, goals, and strategies were then deployed via QFD matrices as illustrated in **Figure S2-2**.

Specific directives that correlate to the strategies were then established:

(Continued on the next page)

		Strategies		
⊚ Strong ○ Medium △ Weak		Implement simultaneous engineering partnerships with suppliers	Apply Taguchi Methods and QFD at the design stage	Institute preventive-maintenance training for customers
Objectives	**Goals**			
Improved product quality and reliability	Reduce number of monthly downtime incidents (mean time between failures)	○	⊚	⊚
	Introduce enhanced flexible manufacturing system	○	⊚	
Reduced delivery times and costs for new products	Reduce delivery time on special orders	⊚	○	
	Obtain cost savings on upgrades of existing products	○	⊚	

Figure S2-2.

Directives

- Establish internal, cross-functional product-development teams
- Revamp the purchasing procedures to encourage innovative working relationships
- Create a service-department arm for preventive maintenance
- Arrange for Taguchi Methods and QFD training for both managers (introductory) and engineers (hands-on)

Using a QFD matrix to deploy these directives creates an "action plan" to help achieve the management-defined strategies. The theory behind this is similar to that of Management by Objectives (MBO), but it is more visually powerful.

	Establish internal, cross-functional product-development teams	Revamp the purchasing procedures to encourage innovative working relationships	Create a service department arm for preventive maintenance	Arrange for Taguchi Methods and QFD training for both managers (introductory) and engineers (hands-on)
Implement simultaneous engineering partnerships with suppliers	◎	◎	△	○
Apply Taguchi Methods and QFD at the design stage	◎	○		◎
Institute preventive-maintenance training for customers			◎	
	Appoint 15 people by Dec. 31	Prepare a prototype purchasing manual by Dec. 31	Assign personnel by Dec. 31	Have 5 managers and 15 engineers trained by Dec. 31

Directives

◎ Strong
○ Medium
△ Weak

Strategies

Measures

Figure S2–3.

Figure S2–3 shows the following measures ("how much" items) for Example 1:

Measures

- Appoint 15 people by December 31
- Prepare a prototype purchasing manual by December 31
- Assign personnel by December 31
- Have 5 managers and 15 engineers trained by December 31

(Continued on the next page)

EXAMPLE 2

Objectives, goals, and strategies identified by the management of a monthly technical journal for business-plan deployment included:

Objectives

- Produce an award-winning monthly technical journal
- Achieve competitive pricing and scheduling for monthly technical journal

Goals

- Improve editorial quality of monthly technical journal
- Improve graphical quality of monthly technical journal
- Reduce composition costs for monthly technical journal
- Shorten production schedule for monthly technical journal

Strategies

- Create an editorial advisory board and institute monthly strategy meetings
- Employ a full-time managing editor
- Invest in an integrated desktop publishing system

QFD was then used to further deploy these objectives, goals, and strategies as shown in **Figure S2–4**.

The following directives were then evolved from the strategies:

		Strategies		
◉ Strong ○ Medium △ Weak Objectives	 Goals	Create an editorial advisory board and institute monthly strategy meetings	Employ a full-time managing editor	Invest in an integrated desktop publishing system
Produce an award-winning monthly technical journal	Improve editorial quality of monthly technical journal	◉	○	
	Improve graphical quality of monthly technical journal	△	○	◉
Achieve competitive pricing and scheduling for monthly technical journal	Reduce composition costs for monthly technical journal		○	◉
	Shorten production schedule for monthly technical journal		○	◉

Figure S2–4.

Directives

- Identify manufacturing managers and engineers for editorial advisory board
- Seek seasoned managing editor with desktop publishing expertise
- Research various integrated desktop publishing systems and make selection
- Prepare a detailed role and mission statement

Figure S2–5 lists the following measures ("how much" items) for Example 2:

(Continued on the next page)

	Directives			
◎ Strong ○ Medium △ Weak Strategies	Identify manufacturing managers and engineers for editorial advisory board	Seek seasoned managing editor with desktop publishing expertise	Research various integrated desktop publishing systems and make selection	Prepare a detailed role and mission statement
Create an editorial advisory board and institute monthly strategy meetings	◎	○		◎
Employ a full-time managing editor		◎		○
Invest in an integrated desktop publishing system		○	◎	
	Appoint 15 people by Dec. 31	Hire a managing editor by Dec. 31	Request competitive bids by Dec. 1, order system by Dec. 31	Submit working document by Dec. 1, final document by Dec. 31

Measures

Figure S2-5.

Measures

- Appoint 15 people by December 31
- Hire a managing editor by December 31
- Request competitive bids by December 1; order system by December 31
- Submit working document by December 1, final document by December 31

QFD can also be used to further deploy these departmental directives into individual work assignments. It can be adapted to meet almost any strategic planning need.

3

The Power of QFD

Quality Function Deployment (QFD) derives much of its strength from its ability to quench an unpopular phenomenon—Murphy's Law. Quite simply, QFD helps keep things from going wrong as a product makes its way through a complicated series of design and production activities.

QFD also addresses the adage "Things that go without saying usually go without doing." By creating a disciplined outline for all involved to follow, QFD enforces efficient information sharing. This, in turn, enhances the product-development process.

Quality Up, Costs Down

QFD can help improve quality while decreasing costs. When it comes to improving competitiveness, cost and quality are determining factors. The idea that costs can be reduced while quality is enhanced, however, isn't always bought by American management.

In a Gallup survey commissioned by the American Society for Quality Control that explored the quality-related attitudes, experiences, and practices of top American management, executives picked "increase employee motivation" over "improvements in quality" as the best way to reduce costs by a two-to-one margin (*Quality Progress*, December 1986).

Policies and techniques that result in high quality at high cost are not representative of keen business acumen—nor are policies and techniques that result in low quality at low cost or, worse yet, low quality at high cost. By using QFD and Taguchi Methods—combined engineering and statistical methods designed to achieve rapid improvements in cost and quality by optimizing product design and manufacturing processes—leading Japanese companies have improved their business operations while improving quality. (Taguchi Methods are described in further detail in the appendix, p. 103).

Affecting both cost and quality is inspection, an expensive, ineffective form of quality control that's both outmoded and counterproductive.

According to "The Push for Quality," a special report published in *BusinessWeek* (June 9, 1987), the typical American factory spends 20-to-50% of its operating budget to find and fix mistakes and as many as one-quarter of all factory hands don't produce anything—they just rework things that weren't done right the first time.

The *BusinessWeek* special report goes on to state that some 80% of quality defects occur during the design phase of product development or as a result of purchasing policies that value low price over the quality of purchased parts and materials. No more than

20% of quality defects occur in response to the production line.

Through the use of QFD, the 80% of quality defects attributed to product design could be substantially reduced. QFD can also be used to initiate a healthy dialogue between purchasing and suppliers aimed at reaching the optimum in product or material cost/quality.

Quality *doesn't* have to equate to high cost. Quality does cost more if it's achieved via inspection. When designed into a product, however, quality reduces costs.

QFD represents a change from the "inspection-rejection-rework-scrap" form of quality control to one that begins at the onset of the product-development process; it replaces the reactive, fire-fighting approach to quality control with one that's proactive—preventive—in nature.

This upstream effort does away with the costly "design-test-fix" scenario, the design counterpart of product inspection. When testing reveals a major flaw in a prototype design, time and dollars are wasted. When this scenario repeats itself two or three times—the dreaded "oh not again" syndrome—the expenditure is doubled or tripled. An adequate design will eventually result, but at great expense. When products are designed, not fixed, to meet customer requirements, costs and product-development cycles are reduced. Inspection to achieve quality is no longer relevant—during product design or manufacture.

According to MIT's Don Clausing, QFD addresses three broad problems attacking American industry: disregard for the voice of the customer, loss of information as a product moves through the product-development cycle, and different interpretations of specifications by the various departments involved. QFD also provides solutions to two problems that are related to those cited above: division by department and sequential timing.

The negative effects of division by department are diminished as QFD is employed horizontally—members of the QFD project team work *together*, not as separate entities. Additionally, QFD's vertical deployment ensures that a concurrent, versus sequential, approach to product development occurs.

One of QFD's most cited benefits is its ability to generate team involvement that's sustained over the entire product-development cycle. The results of this team synergy are much greater than the sum of the team's parts: QFD is a systematic way of bringing the collective wisdom of the corporation to bear on a problem. By pooling the knowledge of the QFD project team, enhanced decision-making occurs; personal biases disappear as the team begins functioning at top capacity.

"The strength of QFD is that the process itself becomes a catalyst that generates team effort and cooperation," says Calvin W. Gray, Group Vice President, Sales and International Operations, Sheller-Globe, Detroit, Michigan. "QFD then becomes a mechanism for communication among the various areas working on the project."

This team approach is fitting with American industry's renewed focus on teams and team building. A small-scale survey of six large manufacturing companies conducted by the Harvard Business School, Boston, Massachusetts, included interviews with 46 "fast-track" managers ("comers") and 14 high-level executives ("incumbents"). The survey's findings, published in *The Uneasy Alliance* (1985, Harvard Business School Press), stated that the comers, in relation to the incumbents, were more participative, interested in team building and collaboration, and critical of their company's lack of communication.

Short-term benefits afforded by QFD include shorter product-development cycles, fewer design changes, fewer start-up problems, improved quality and reliability, and cost savings through product- and process-design optimization.

For example, Toyota Auto Body Co., Ltd., Kariya, Japan, reported a cumulative 61% reduction in start-up costs related to the introduction of four van models from January 1977 to April 1984 (see **Figure 3–1**). The product-development cycle during this same time frame was reduced by one-third. Quality improvements were cited as well.

In addition, numerous Toyota suppliers have reported that implementation of QFD has improved quality while reducing costs, cut product-development times in half, and helped achieve major competitive advantages.

The Voice of the Customer Speaks

Customer requirements can be easily misinterpreted during the complicated product-development cycle. For example, the marketing manager may ask for "understated opulence." To the design engineer, however, "understated" or, for that matter, "opulent" may have a completely different meaning. The QFD

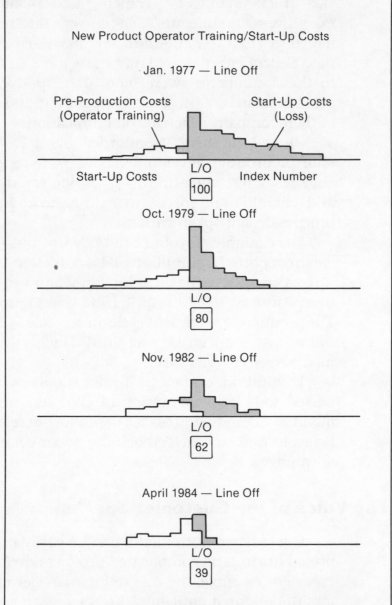

Figure 3-1. Toyota Auto Body reported a cumulative 61% reduction in start-up costs for four van models (1977-84) through the use of QFD.

process translates the customer's message in its purest form, without the ambiguity caused by multiple interpretations.

QFD not only focuses company-wide attention on customer requirements, it also provides a mechanism to target selected areas where competitive advantages could help improve market share—areas with undeveloped potential. By identifying critical design and part characteristics—the characteristics that have the greatest influence on overall customer requirements—QFD ensures that product-development efforts yield the most bang for the buck.

QFD can also be used to lower warranty costs on existing products, which has a positive effect on profitability. One of the most widely presented QFD applications, the Toyota Auto Body rust case study, was initiated in response to escalating warranty costs due to corrosion. Through the use of QFD and Taguchi Methods, Toyota virtually eliminated its corrosion-warranty expense.

Creating a Knowledge Base

After the efforts of a QFD project have been deemed successful, the *knowledge base* created for that project serves as a repository for engineering knowledge.

With QFD, knowledge can be preserved in one concise place, in contrast to unruly design-standards manuals. The matrices and charts prepared during the QFD procedure create a working document that can be easily referenced and learned from.

The QFD knowledge base holds great promise for future product-development efforts. It holds the an-

Why QFD?

Tangible benefits

- Major reduction in development time
- Virtual elimination of late engineering changes
- Lower-cost designs at the outset
- Enhanced design reliability
- Economical factory controls

Intangible benefits

- Increased customer satisfaction
- Stable quality-assurance planning activity
- QFD documentation package
    - —Often applies to generic family
    - —Transferable storehouse of engineering know-how
- Basis for improvement planning

Summary value

- Strengthens current development process
    - —Clear targets defined early based on market/business demands
    - —Simultaneous focus on product and process technologies
    - —Key issues remain visible for prioritizing resource allocation
    - —Communication and teamwork are enhanced
- Desired output efficiently achieved
    - —Products meet customers' needs
    - —Products provide a competitive edge

—Excerpted from "Putting the Quality Function Deployment Concept to Work," presented by George R. Perry, Vice President, Quality and Reliability, Allied-Signal, Inc., Southfield, Michigan, at the 25th Annual Fall Conference of the ASQC Automotive Division.

swers to questions concerning what decisions were made and why—and can simplify similar decision-making endeavors. Concurrently, it helps prevent problems that occurred in 1987 from recurring in 1992.

In addition, QFD can be used to train entry-level engineers. By reviewing the results of successful QFD projects, entry-level engineers begin higher up on the learning curve. The process also offers potential for continuing education of employees across departmental lines.

"QFD will provide us with a database for design engineering of future products," explains Sheller-Globe's Calvin W. Gray. "We initially expect that it will consume more man-hours, from an engineering-talent standpoint, to complete a successful QFD project. But when we do a similar product down the road, the time required to gain the same level of product quality will be reduced. The net result will be a significant reduction of time from product conception to introduction in the field."

The Budd Co.'s Norman E. Morrell agrees: "QFD lays a foundation for future work—you don't have to continually reinvent the wheel or wonder how you did it last time. It also provides a needed discipline, much like a pilot's checklist. A guy may have flown 300 missions, but he still checks off every instrument when he gets into that cockpit."

Also in agreement is Nakahita Sato, a director at Toyota Auto Body: "QFD appears complicated at first glance, and technical personnel might tend to respectfully ignore it, but the data can be considered as an accumulation of the know-how of the past that can be added to or improved with each new development cycle and, therefore, becomes an important asset of the company.

"Today, when the number of projects is increasing annually, even technical personnel with comparatively little experience often have an opportunity to work at the first level of responsibility. By the use of this method, perhaps it will be possible for them to work even better while simultaneously taking advantage of the knowledge of experienced personnel." At Toyota Auto Body, QFD is used to make good engineers great engineers.

Integrating Process and Design

QFD can be thought of as the glue that binds the various product-development stages together: By tying design and process activities together, it provides integration of the various functions.

Raymond P. Smock, Manager, Advanced Quality Concepts Development, Product Assurance, Ford Motor Co., Dearborn, Michigan, describes QFD as an all-encompassing planning framework for product development. "QFD integrates the process by which you translate customer requirements into technical requirements for each stage of product development," he explains. "QFD prioritizes product and manufacturing-process characteristics and highlights areas requiring further analysis."

In Smock's opinion, QFD is of greatest benefit when applied to complex systems that don't lend themselves to such traditional approaches as rule-based design.

QFD is being taught at the Ford Motor Co. in conjunction with a Company-Wide Quality Control

(CWQC) training program begun in June 1987. The groundwork for this program—which is the result of extensive study and evaluation—began in the early 1980s, when quality guru Dr. W. Edwards Deming visited Ford, followed by Japanese CWQC authority Dr. Kaoru Ishikawa.

QFD is highly complementary to CWQC or Total Quality Control (TQC) programs, as well as simultaneous engineering partnerships. In many ways, the QFD approach is a logical extension of simultaneous engineering—it promotes the same up-front team approach to concurrent product development while placing increased emphasis on the voice of the customer and providing detailed documentation of the team's efforts.

How important is QFD to a total quality program? When asked what elements led to the quality transformation at Toyota Auto Body, the CJQCA's Akashi Fukuhara named Taguchi Methods, Fault-Tree Analysis (FTA) and Reverse Fault-Tree Analysis (RFTA), Failure-Mode and Effect Analysis (FMEA), Statistical Process Control (SPC), and QFD. (Fukuhara worked at Toyota Auto Body for some 20 years and was instrumental in instituting TQC at the company.)

Fukuhara was also asked to rate the importance of each of these tools to quality improvement at Toyota Auto Body. He made the following estimates: Taguchi Methods, 50%; FTA/RFTA, 35%; and FMEA, 15%—which together total 100%! SPC, he explained, was used to monitor, maintain, and uplift quality, rather than for actual quality improvement. This doesn't mean that SPC shouldn't be used for quality improvement in America, but that *Toyota's* processes no longer require the use of SPC for quality improve-

Comments from the Field

"The need for QFD is best summed up by the statement 'get better or get beat.' QFD will simply improve and focus new-product-development activities by getting the whole organization to concentrate on rapid development of new products with high quality and low cost."
—Michael E. Chupa, Vice President of Marketing, ITT Hancock, Jackson, Michigan

"QFD helps tie product design and process activities together—it provides better integration of the various functions. It's a systematic way of bringing the collective wisdom of the corporation to bear on the problem."
—Dr. Don Clausing, Bernard Gordon Adjunct Professor of Engineering Innovation and Practice, Massachusetts Institute of Technology, Cambridge, Massachusetts

"We can't improve quality by continuing to reactively fix problems. QFD gives us an opportunity to stop talking about fixing and start talking about preventing."
—Robert J. Dika, Specialist, Engineering Quality Assurance, Chrysler Corp., Highland Park, Michigan

"QFD formalizes your product-development process and the record-keeping that goes along with it. This helps everybody understand just what the process entails."
—James T. Gipprich, Director, Market Development, Kelsey-Hayes Co., Romulus, Michigan

"What's the single greatest strength the Japanese have gained from using QFD? Ensuring that the product they deliver to the market comes the closest to fulfilling all needs the customer might experience."

> —Calvin W. Gray, Group Vice President, Sales and International Operations, Sheller-Globe, Detroit, Michigan

"As a professor, I'm always looking for concepts that are teachable. QFD is a teachable discipline. One can teach it in a classroom or elsewhere, providing people with the basis for getting started or changing the way they do these activities."

> —Walton M. Hancock, Associate Dean, Center for Research on Integrated Manufacturing, College of Engineering, University of Michigan, Ann Arbor, Michigan

"QFD is an excellent planning tool—a vehicle by which we can get people working together as a team to reach common goals. It's a tool that ensures that all bases are covered, that no stone is left unturned."

> —Norman E. Morrell, Corporate Manager, Quality-Product Reliability, The Budd Co., Troy, Michigan

"QFD offers many benefits for the ultimate consumer because of what it accomplishes up front. With QFD, there's no need to put on bandages. Doing so usually costs everybody money—despite all efforts to ensure that those bandages solve the problem, weaknesses generally exist. The ultimate customer suffers in the long run, as does the company's reputation."

> —George R. Perry, Vice President, Quality and Reliability, Allied-Signal, Inc., Automotive Sector World Headquarters, Southfield, Michigan

(Continued on the next page)

Comments from the Field (continued)

"QFD forces people to be more conscious of potential problems and, as a result, to do a better job. Not only will QFD help us find the holes, it will help us from repeating past mistakes."

> —Robert H. Schaefer, Reliability Engineering Director, Product Assurance and Validation, Chevrolet-Pontiac-Canada Group, General Motors Corp., Warren, Michigan

"QFD will point you toward the areas where you need to do further analytical work—it results in more focused analyses aimed at meeting customer requirements. This is a major breakthrough. People are searching for where to use analytical tools, such as design of experiments. QFD leads the way."

> —Raymond P. Smock, Manager, Advanced Quality Concepts Development, Product Assurance, Ford North American Automotive Operations, Dearborn, Michigan

"One of QFD's biggest merits is in supplying new employees with the background and experience gained by their predecessors. Internally, we see a smoother transition through QFD and, therefore, reduced lead times for new designs. In addition, the products we manufacture will be of higher quality."

> —Peter J. Soltis, Senior Technical Specialist, Product Engineering, Kelsey-Hayes Co., Romulus, Michigan

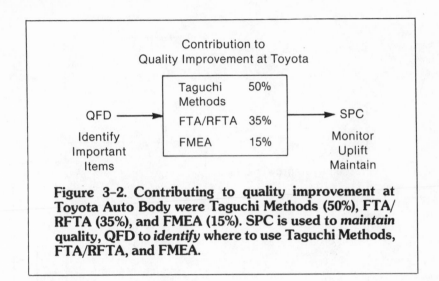

Figure 3–2. Contributing to quality improvement at Toyota Auto Body were Taguchi Methods (50%), FTA/RFTA (35%), and FMEA (15%). SPC is used to *maintain* quality, QFD to *identify* where to use Taguchi Methods, FTA/RFTA, and FMEA.

ment. QFD, on the other hand, was the map that identified when and where to apply the above tools (see **Figure 3–2**).

QFD helps identify which analytical tools (Taguchi Methods, FTA, RFTA, FMEA, and so forth) would be best utilized during the product-development cycle, as well as conflicting design requirements that would benefit from optimization (see the appendix on p. 103 for a brief description of Taguchi Methods and parameter design). This feed-forward mechanism captures knowledge that might otherwise go undocumented (see **Figure 3–3**). The Japanese religiously use QFD in conjunction with Taguchi Methods and other quality-control technologies, capitalizing on the benefits of each.

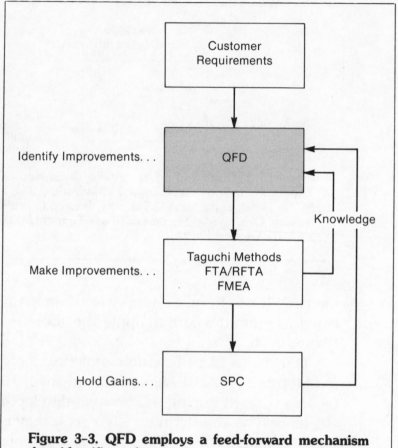

Figure 3–3. QFD employs a feed-forward mechanism that identifies where to use such tools as Taguchi Methods, FTA/RFTA, FMEA, and SPC and then documents their use.

4

Sizing Up the Competition

Traditional distinctions between domestic and foreign competition are becoming increasingly blurred as the multinational company comes of age. The management of many foreign companies acknowledges this fact. Consequently, these companies are making moves to enhance their international presence—including more direct investing on North American soil. The by-products of this investment are becoming increasingly visible. Today, direct foreign investment into the United States amounts to about $200 billion, spurring business expansion, new factories, and new American jobs. By the mid-1990s, it's projected that foreign investors, led by the Japanese, could own some $400 billion worth of American factories—double what they own today.

Encouraging direct foreign investment are trade friction and the threat of protectionist measures. When confronted with trade quotas and the like, foreign companies are replacing exports with local production bases. The end result will be maintained or expanded U.S. market shares and increased competition for U.S. companies.

According to Tokyo's Ministry of International Trade and Industry, Japanese investment will create more than 840,000 American jobs in the next decade. This will reduce the revenue of American companies while furthering the need for increased labor efficiency, all of which puts industrial America in a venue of change and creates new and greater challenges.

Advantage from Adversity

These challenges also present several opportunities—the opportunity to perfect American management and manufacturing practices, the opportunity to satisfy customer and company requirements simultaneously, the opportunity to manufacture products at lower cost with higher quality, and the opportunity to manufacture such products sooner than the competition.

Quality Function Deployment (QFD) can help turn these opportunities into realities by reducing the time needed to bring a product to market by one-third to half—which will reduce total product cost and result in a more timely, competitive product—and by reducing material costs and overhead, the two highest contributors to total manufacturing costs. QFD does so by minimizing engineering changes within the product-development cycle and by ensuring that required changes occur on paper rather than hardware.

To quote Walton M. Hancock, Associate Dean, Center for Research on Integrated Manufacturing, College of Engineering, University of Michigan, Ann

Arbor, Michigan, "We have to really focus our ability to produce high-quality products at low cost and to produce products people want to buy in a world market. The combination of the two together is very crucial. The ability to produce things people want to buy in a world market means that products have to be designed so that people worldwide will want them—not just people in the U.S. The other issue is the ability to change products quickly—if your competitor comes out with something better, you'd better be able to react to it."

The road to a global marketplace, however, isn't paved with gold or without stones or forks. Included in the last category is the issue of protectionism, which met with little favor in a 1987 survey released by Coopers & Lybrand, New York, a Big Eight public accounting, tax, and management consulting firm.

Coopers & Lybrand's study, titled "Made in America: A Survey of Manufacturing's Future," consisted of in-depth interviews with 301 top manufacturing executives at Fortune 500 companies and 351 "knowledge workers" (engineers who spend at least 25% of their professional time on the operating floor of a manufacturing facility or are primarily involved in product or process design).

Only 10% of the surveyed executives think import restrictions would be an effective way of restoring their competitive position. This is good news to America's multinational companies, many of which are drawing good percentages of sales from abroad.

Other executives, as well as politicians, repeatedly stress that countries that export to America must also be prepared to open their markets and import American-made products. Political pressures seem to preclude such a scenario. Quality and cost requirements, however, will be just as stringent overseas as they are on domestic soil. We think that market barriers are our major hindrance, but in many instances our products themselves are standing in the way.

A Global Perspective?

Although the message to industrial America is a global one, not all American companies are taking it seriously. According to the Coopers & Lybrand study, most American manufacturing companies still view other domestic companies as their primary competition—despite well-publicized concern for American manufacturing's global competitiveness.

Of the executives surveyed for the "Made in America" study, 55% see their toughest competition coming from companies within the U.S., 13% from Japan, 13% from the Pacific Basin, 11% from Western Europe, and 2% from Latin America (see **Figure 4–1**). Thirty-six percent of these same executives foresee that by 1992 their competition will come from domestic companies, 20% from Japan, 18% from the Pacific Basin, 10% from Western Europe, and 6% from Latin America (see **Figure 4–2**). Establishing a competitive international position was judged a serious problem by 44% of the executives interviewed.

"The optimism expressed by these top manufacturing executives reveals a certain myopia. Although perceiving growing competition from abroad, manufacturers still see the main competition coming from across the street, rather than from across the ocean," says Henry Johansson, Chairman of Coopers & Ly-

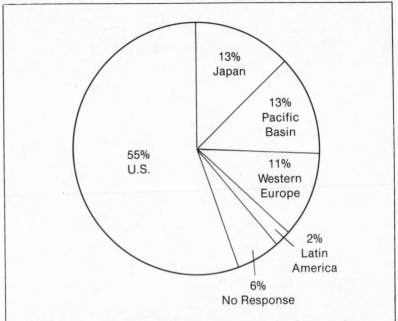

Figure 4–1. Fifty-five percent of the surveyed executives see their toughest competition coming from companies within the U.S., 13% from Japan, 13% from the Pacific Basin, 11% from Western Europe, and 2% from Latin America (6%, no response).

brand's Manufacturing Industry practice. "Lessons that should have been learned from autos, steel, and machine tools have been lost on other manufacturing segments, and rather than taking a global view, the executives still tend to think and plan domestically."

According to Johansson, the surveyed executives seem to be looking at domestic competition as the most important gauge for success. They're primarily using American market share as a measure, while it's clear that almost every American industry participates in a global market.

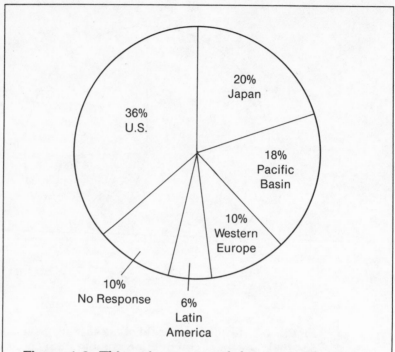

Figure 4–2. Thirty-six percent of the surveyed executives foresee their toughest competition coming from within the U.S., 20% from Japan, 18% from the Pacific Basin, 10% from Western Europe, and 6% from Latin America by 1992 (10%, no response).

Industries Under Attack

A number of American industries have been adversely affected by lower-cost, higher-quality imports—including the apparel, automotive, camera, consumer electronics, earth-moving equipment, heavy truck, machine tool, small-gasoline-engine equipment, steel, and textile industries. A few have been crippled so badly that recovery seems doubtful. The threat doesn't come just from the Japanese—numerous Southeast Asian and European companies are reaping the profits of increased market share and are forces to be reckoned with as well.

"Price, delivery time, reliability. For nearly ten years U.S. machine-tool manufacturers have been getting beaten by the Japanese on all three counts. In recent years, Taiwan and South Korea have entered the fray, using well-made, low-cost machines to capture segments of the U.S. market," writes Gregory T. Farnum in "The Machine Tool Industry—A Look Ahead" (*Manufacturing Engineering*, November 1986). "And behind the Taiwanese and Koreans loom an array of new competitors, some of them from countries many Americans would have a tough time locating on a map. The result: Imports now account for more than half of U.S. machine-tool consumption."

This is just one example of a once-sluggish Japanese industry that's received new life. Machine tools are produced in Japan in greater quantities than in any other country. In 1955, however, this wasn't the case. The technical level of Japanese machine tools was considered more than 20 years behind those manufactured in the U.S. and Europe. Additionally, 30-to-50% of the Japanese machine-tool supply was imported. Today, computer-numerical-control Japanese machine tools are both technologically advanced and popular on the home front.

The automotive industry, too, is still being plagued by the effects of globalization. *Changing Alliances* by Davis Dyer, Malcolm S. Salter, and Alan M. Webber (1987, Harvard Business School Press), published as a result of the "Harvard Business School Project on the Auto Industry and the American Economy," reports that globalization poses a direct challenge to both the American automotive industry and the American economy—because the American system has a fundamental disadvantage in a free world market. Other industries will experience similar plights as well, as globalization sweeps American industries, the study reports.

An appendix to *Changing Alliances*, "Competitive Product Programs and Anticipated Domestic Production and Auto-related Employment for 1990," prepared by John O'Donnell, states that Japanese automakers have captured almost 50% of the U.S. small-car market, nearly 25% of the mid-size-car market, and more than 40% of the sports-car market. The appendix also reveals that from 1980 to 1985, Japanese and Korean automakers introduced five times as many new small cars as American automakers, three times as many mid-size cars, and twice as many new sports cars. That's the beauty of shortened product cycles.

In addition, the Japanese are continually targeting new niches for entry that have traditionally been dominated by industrial America and are beefing up other industries in response to competitive pressures from other countries. The 1986 *Japan Economic Almanac* identifies the computer and chemical industries as industries characterized by excellent growth potential. The almanac also reports that Japanese affiliates of American companies in the computer industry were touted for their use of advanced technology, but saw little growth in sales because their products failed to decipher Japanese characters—an example of not meeting the voice of the customer.

Heeding the Warning

The Coopers & Lybrand study "Made in America" reports that a majority of the surveyed executives think the U.S. could regain competitive advantage in automobiles (88%), steel (71%), and machine tools (66%). Of the 301 manufacturing executives surveyed, 66% think the U.S. will reverse any competitive disadvantage it now has, and 67% of the knowledge workers reiterated their position.

Do industry facts and findings support such optimism? Not necessarily. While direct foreign investment has been credited with making for more equalized operating conditions, it will also result in more capacity. Foreign competition isn't going to go away—the Japanese and other competitors are going to continue to streamline operations in pursuit of cost reductions and value-added advantages. Also, excess capacity exists in many areas, such as the automotive and microelectronics industries.

A special report published in *Fortune* (February 2, 1987), "The Economy of the 1990s," projected that foreign automotive companies will at least double their current output of 600,000 cars in America as at least six new plants become operational. Some industry estimates indicate that Japanese automakers will have the capacity to make about two million cars at North American plants by 1990, resulting in an excess of more than 4.5 million cars in the U.S. Most Japanese automotive companies with American factories are already boosting production—the remainder plan to have their American plants start operations before 1990. And foreign automotive suppliers have begun to—and will surely continue to—follow suit, as will manufacturers and suppliers in other industries.

The time to take a tough, competitive stance, using sure-fire technical and managerial tools when and where needed, is upon us.

5

Wherein Lies the Difference?

The charge is a serious one: American product development is driven by the voice of the engineer and the voice of the executive, not the voice of the customer. There is an opinion, however, that this is changing. From corporate directives to national advertising, the message is a customer-driven one. Customer requirements must come first.

Take, for example, the mission statement prepared by Kelsey-Hayes Co., Romulus, Michigan, as part of its company-wide excellence program: "The Kelsey-Hayes Co. mission is to be the best supplier of products and services to our customers. We will accomplish this through the dedicated efforts of our employees and by effectively using all resources within the corporation. Our success will result in growth and prosperity." Guiding principles behind the Kelsey-Hayes mission include "Customers are the focus of everything we do," "Continuous improvement is essential to our success," and "Suppliers are our partners."

In Retrospect

Is the voice of the customer really that important? In addition to slipping market shares, the circumstances surrounding the May 17, 1987, Iraqi jet attack on the USS *Stark*—which killed 37 American sailors— reminds us that it is. When a radar operator became annoyed by the beep of an electronic warning system designed to alert the *Stark* crew of hostile radar, he turned the system's audible signal off. The system's visual signal wasn't detected in time, and the *Stark* tragedy is being partially blamed on human error. That human error, however, resulted from an unhappy customer.

"The tale is a nightmare for the manufacturers of sophisticated electronic weaponry, who find increasingly that the systems they are building have become too complex for soldiers and sailors to operate properly," writes John H. Cushman Jr. in the *New York Times* (June 21, 1987). "Moreover, maintenance and repair of the electronic weapons are also often beyond the ability of most military personnel, despite the investment of enormous amounts of training time, according to experts both inside and outside the government."

What Went Wrong?

Industry gurus have earmarked a number of inefficiencies that result in unmet customer needs. Planning—although usually performed with the best intentions—is performed in haste. This occurs because planning is performed under the restraints of a conflicting message: It's important to plan but nonproductive to do so. Consequently, planning provides general direction but little attention to detail, which is left to the execution stage. There's no time to do things right—but plenty of time to do things over.

Objectives receive similar handling. Objectives are generally construed as worthwhile goals—but the means to achieve them are often unclear. Differences in interpretations and priorities, hidden conflicts, etc., all add up to objectives that aren't clearly defined.

Product-development inefficiencies and manufacturing inefficiencies don't help, either. The former include losing sight of the customer, preoccupation with the schedule versus the product, inadequate front-loading, improper use of product testing, new but not better designs, preoccupation with design changes, isolation of design efforts, designing and building to specification tolerances versus target values, inadequate consideration of manufacturing needs, and achievement of sensitive optimums. The latter include inefficient manufacturing processes, excessive inventories, added cost to improve quality, and dependence on operator-sensitive procedures. Focusing on short-term problem solving and using high technology for problem solving result in additional roadblocks. **Figure 5-1** contrasts this problem-solving approach with the Japanese approach of problem prevention.

MIT's Don Clausing has identified ten cash drains that plague American industry:

- **Technology push—but where's the pull?:** The United States is very good at technology genera-

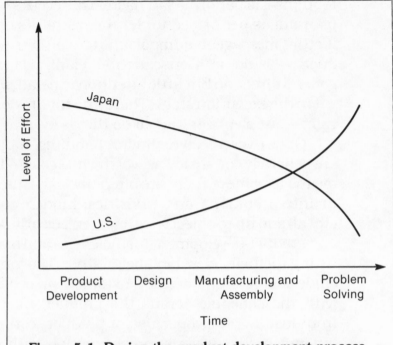

Figure 5-1. During the product-development process, Japanese engineers focus their efforts on such upstream activities as research and development and design. U.S. engineers, on the other hand, typically concentrate on problem-solving activities.

tion. But a threefold problem exists: new technological concepts are developed and major resources spent, but no discernable customer need can be identified; strong customer needs exist for which technology-generation activities are lacking; and good technological concepts are developed for which there are clear customer needs, but these concepts are inadequately transferred into system-design activities.

- **Disregard for the voice of the customer:** Products are often doomed to mediocrity at the first step of system design—determination of customer needs. Contributing to this failure is emphasis on the voice of the executive or the voice of the engineer, rather than the voice of the customer.

- **The "great idea":** Product-concept selection often results after someone shouts, "I have this great idea!" This concept then becomes the only concept given serious consideration, although it may be highly vulnerable and unable to withstand the test of time.

- **Pretend designs:** Pretend designs are new but not better product designs. Often, they're not production-intent designs, focusing instead on the creation of experimental prototypes. A lack of production intention leads to a disastrous attitude, "This is just a first design—I'll fix it later."

- **Pampered products:** Product concepts are often pampered so they look good in demonstration. This approach has been improved upon by rigorous application of reliability growth and problem-solving methodologies. These, however, aren't adequate approaches to optimization of vital design parameters.

- **Hardware swamps:** Hardware swamps occur when prototypes are so numerous, with overlapping test phases, that excessive time is spent debugging and maintaining them, rather than improving the product design.

- **"Here's the product, where's the factory?":** If production-capability design starts only a few months before actual production, many severe problems will occur.

- **"We've always made it this way":** Process-operating points (speeds, depth of cut, feed rates, pressures, temperatures, etc.) are specified on process sheets or numerical-control programs. Process-parameter values have often been fixed for a long time and may have resulted from little, if any, development. This leads to a dangerous attitude, "We've always made it this way and it works." This, in turn, leads to reliance on tradition versus innovation.
- **Inspection:** Factory inspection—sorting the good products from the bad after production is complete—is an inefficient process. The same holds for product testing (design inspection) during development.
- **"Give me my targets, let me do my thing":** Early allocation of targets to a detailed level tends to destroy teamwork. Contracts where each person works in isolation lead to subsystems that can't be integrated, products that can't be produced, production capacity that can't produce modern products, operating systems that attempt to enslave their users, managers who can't manage, and employees who wait to be told what to do.

According to Clausing, an improved total-development process—which includes QFD—aimed at continuously bringing better products to market will plug the cash drains.

"One difficulty is getting people to admit that there are problems in the work process. But the thought is slowly permeating American industry that our work process needs improving," says Clausing.

"The Japanese had change forced upon them—they knew they had to improve. They're very oriented toward things like continuous improvement, which QFD helps bring about."

A Revised Approach

Documentation of how the Japanese turned their manufacturing operations around was zealously sought after from the mid-1970s on. With this pursuit came a greater understanding of Japan's industrial rejuvenation and the operating differences between Japanese and U.S. companies (see **Figure 5-2**). The Japanese did more than copy Western managerial and technological concepts and techniques: They religiously studied these tools and selectively applied the ones that seemed to work best—and were best suited to their specific cultural environment.

The Japanese didn't set out to become inventors. Rather, their approach smacked of common sense—with a bit of innovation added for good measure. The managerial- and manufacturing-related procedures being debated weren't new to the manufacturing realm. When deemed appropriate to the situation, they were applied. When not deemed appropriate, they were discarded. Many could just as easily have been applied in the U.S. or another country. Application of others would have required a bit more forethought—in some cases, cultural aspirations and expectations might have nullified their effectiveness.

The use of Statistical Quality Control (SQC) and Statistical Process Control (SPC) had many merits; the use of extensive work-in-process inventories did not. The teachings of Dr. W. Edwards Deming and Dr.

Operating Differences	
Japan	U.S.
Deploy the voice of the customer (decide what is important)	Specify internal requirements (everything is important)
Design and build to target values (reduce variation or dispersion)	Design and build to specification tolerances (manage around tolerance stack)
Optimize product and process design	React to customer problems

Figure 5–2. A number of operating differences exist between Japanese and U.S. companies; in particular, identifying and deploying customer requirements (QFD) and optimizing product and process design (Taguchi Methods).

Joseph M. Juran were put into practice; Just-in-Time Manufacturing would later be applied. Teamwork, consensus, and organization were desirable. Irrationally complex systems were not. Manufacturers began working in concert with unions, suppliers, and government; simplicity became a word to work by.

The results of the Japanese effort included improved scheduling/production-control systems, process technologies, quality systems and procedures, internal communications, and problem-solving techniques. By fashioning a management and engineering philosophy that produced quality products with reduced variation through optimized design and improved processes, Japanese companies accumulated market share.

It was—and is—a long-term effort that results in continuous quality improvement. What began with quality improvement through statistical quality methods evolved into Total Quality Control (TQC), which itself matured to become today's Company-Wide Quality Control (CWQC).

Just as the Japanese incorporated Western concepts and techniques, Americans can apply the same selective-reasoning process to Japanese tools, tailoring them to American needs and improving them wherever possible. For example, ITT Mechanical Systems and Components-N.A., Bloomfield Hills, Michigan, is using a three-phase QFD procedure, which shortens the time needed to successfully implement the methodology. Other improvements are being contemplated by other QFD pioneers as well.

Application of Japanese-inspired managerial and manufacturing techniques in the U.S. should be part of a systematic effort—a planned endeavor that's analyzed and evaluated on the basis of current company needs and strategies. As Allied-Signal's George R. Perry aptly puts it, "One of the roles I have in my job is to continue to search out, review, and evaluate new concepts and methods for quality improvement. If they seem to be in line with our strategic initiatives or will enhance our ability to move forward, that information is transferred to our operating divisions worldwide." In that capacity and through involvement in seminars, conferences, and study missions, Perry was introduced to QFD.

The Role of QFD

When Japanese companies deploy the voice of the customer, they mobilize all employees to focus on continuous quality improvement with reduced costs and faster response times. In the broadest sense, CWQC refers to quality of management, human behavior, work performance, work environment, products, and service—which, combined, encompass quality of society, industries, the national economy, and global competition.

For maximum long-term benefit, QFD should be applied as the main product-development thrust of CWQC. QFD shouldn't be used on every part of every product—not necessarily even on every product. To do so would defeat one of QFD's main thrusts—bringing a high-quality product to market in as short a time span as practical. Instead, priority is given to parts and functions with the most potential for improved competitive advantage.

QFD is used to identify and focus on the high-risk details of product development. The normal operating system at the typical American company can successfully handle the majority of production-development details—we needn't belabor them with QFD. QFD should be applied on the product aspects that our normal system fails to ensure—problem areas and implementation of innovations.

In Japan, QFD is often applied in conjunction with a specific company-wide theme, such as reducing product-development time, reducing product defects, and so forth. According to the CJQCA's Akashi Fukuhara, most Japanese winners of the Deming Application Prize—awarded to the competing company that achieves the most distinctive improvement of performance through the application of SQC in a designated year—use QFD.

6

Getting Started

Quality Function Deployment (QFD) is still in the infancy stage in the United States. The challenge for American companies is to consistently use QFD to the utmost advantage—and to find new ways of doing so. The majority of the QFD pioneers interviewed for this book indicated that QFD is still in the learning-curve stage at their respective companies. This doesn't mean that they aren't committed to it; on the contrary, they're taking the time to thoroughly assimilate the process in order to achieve lasting results. They realize that implementing QFD at Toyota Auto Body took a good number of years, and that long-term improvement is never easy.

Most of these QFD proponents learned of the process through seminars or study missions to Japan. All expressed enthusiasm for the process; all cautioned that putting QFD to work in the U.S. won't be easy, that doing so will require demonstrated organizational change.

"Many companies think they're ready for this type of change," explains Sheller-Globe's Calvin W. Gray. "But when it comes time to practice it, they don't really sign up. Everybody is for improvement—but they're not always ready to make the changes that must precede improvement. It's important for management to understand that change may be required to successfully implement QFD."

And while the interviewees have their roots in the automotive industry, where QFD was first introduced, interest in the process spans a wide array of industries and applications.

A Team Effort

QFD is designed to be a team activity, from the initial brainstorming of customer requirements through the deployment of those requirements. Because of the emphasis QFD places on the team, it's complementary to comprehensive, company-wide planning efforts and simultaneous engineering partnerships.

According to the CJQCA's Akashi Fukuhara, who consults regularly with U.S. companies on the implementation of QFD, manufacturing must be more consistently drawn into the total product-development process. "Most of the U.S. companies I've talked to have only involved quality assurance and design people—manufacturing and manufacturing engineering people are not yet involved in the QFD process," he explains.

"Getting the operations people to come to the party is a bit of a problem," agrees Robert H. Schaefer, Reliability Engineering Director, Product Assurance and Validation, Chevrolet-Pontiac-Canada Group, General Motors Corp., Warren, Michigan. "Right now, QFD is more engineering-driven. But manufacturing is beginning to participate. We've got some people within the manufacturing organization who are totally obsessed with it."

Multidisciplinary teams should consist of approximately five to seven people, with all key functions represented. The project leader should be skilled in coordination, not domination. QFD is consensus-oriented and excels in a creative, "free-wheeling" environment.

Major projects will probably require some 50 to 60 hours of meetings, which are used to coordinate activities and update matrices and charts. Team members will also spend much time outside of meetings at work on individual assignments. Much of what they'll do will be part of their regular job assignments—directed by the QFD planning effort.

There are several key points the QFD project team should remember. The process may look easy—but it requires effort. Many of the entries may look obvious—after they're written down. The charts may appear to be the objective—rather, they're the means of achieving the objective. The objective is identifying and deploying the voice of the customer.

Selecting a project that's manageable and supported by management and peers will also help get QFD off to a good start. It's best to begin with a project that's small enough to follow through to completion: Success on a small scale always beats failure on a large scale. In general, QFD is usually selectively applied to components or systems that call for a marketing or competitive advantage.

The First Steps

What young America drinks is very important to Bacardi Imports, Inc., American marketer and distributor of Bacardi rum—patrons of trendy bars nationwide periodically include Bacardi Imports employees keeping tabs on who's drinking what.

Japanese automakers, too, send employees to the field—to auto shows, for example—in search of customer-oriented clues that help define what the competition's up to and what the customer likes best. Places like Tokyo's Akihabara, an electronics test-market haven, serve a similar function. Field work can yield important insight into the voice of the customer.

More analytical approaches to obtaining the voice of the customer should also be used in conjunction with QFD. How different is this initial collection of data from traditional marketing techniques?

"Marketing people often study the same problems but they use different techniques," explains Donald R. Bacon, a marketing doctoral student at the University of Michigan, Ann Arbor, Michigan, who also holds a B.S.M.E. and an M.B.A. "Marketing has a long tradition of how to do marketing research. QFD has come along more recently from an entirely different body of knowledge. There are some basic differences, but they're moving toward exactly the same goal—better understanding the needs of the consumer and building that into the product." In general, QFD is more of a qualitative approach, traditional marketing more quantitative.

Understanding and applying the needs of the customer is embodied in the System 4 garment bag designed by the Samsonite Division of Beatrice Companies in the mid-1980s (*Sales & Marketing Management*, September 1986). After setting out to develop innovative new products with patented features, Samsonite launched an extensive consumer research program. Some 400 consumers were initially asked what problems they had experienced with their luggage; another 400 consumers were then asked to rank the problems by severity. This resulted in a new garment-bag design, which was also subjected to a consumer survey—some 3,000 consumers ultimately participated in Samsonite's consumer research. The finished product, the System 4 garment bag, was an instantaneous market success. By becoming more consumer-conscious, Samsonite was again number one in the American luggage market.

Whether acquired via field work or other forms of marketing analysis, true customer requirements— requirements that are clearly expressed in layman's terms—must be acquired before QFD can begin. Without a true understanding of the voice of the customer, QFD can become a futile exercise. Achieving an understanding of the voice of the customer isn't always as easy as it sounds. Once achieved, however, it sets the stage for a successful QFD application.

The Kelsey-Hayes Co., Romulus, Michigan, like The Budd Co., answered ASI's call for QFD case studies in late 1985. Kelsey-Hayes' first QFD application, a House of Quality for a coolant-level sensor being developed for Ford Motor Co. (see sidebar, "Success in the U.S.," p. 28 in Chapter 2), was critiqued during the 1986 ASI study mission to Japan. That led to subsequent QFD charts and a second QFD case study. The second QFD application, a power-door-lock actuator, entailed extensive brainstorming and review of marketing data.

"We were basically looking at two customers, Ford Motor Co. and the person who drives the car. We really wanted to identify the needs of the person who uses the total system—not only our component, which is installed within the door," explains James T. Gipprich, Director, Market Development, Kelsey-Hayes Co.

"Our team started by identifying what we thought were the customer requirements. Next, we put those requirements in a questionnaire and had people comment on them. That's when we found out that what we thought were appropriate questions didn't make a lot of sense to the average person driving a car."

Once the questions were reworded, the joint Kelsey-Hayes/Ford Motor Co. project got well under way. It was a concerted team effort that included two-hour biweekly meetings with well-planned agendas.

GM's Schaefer also stresses the importance of a crystal-clear interpretation: "The secret is to capture the voice of the customer in such a manner that the engineer knows what to do with it and unleashes creative energies in answer to customer needs. The engineer doesn't really need that interpretation from marketing—it's far better that he or she hears what the customer is saying. That's step one. If you haven't done that step properly, the rest of your QFD project will be questionable."

"Going into any study, you should have some hypothesis that you'd like to test. If you go into it blindly you'll most likely flounder around. It's best to have an objective that's clearly stated up front," adds Bacon.

As explained in Chapter 2, a series of steps follow determination of customer requirements: determining design requirements, relating customer and design requirements, evaluating the competition, prioritizing efforts, identifying and resolving trade-offs, determining measures of design requirements, and completing subsequent QFD matrices and charts.

These matrices and charts can be completed by hand or by computer. The Kelsey-Hayes Co. chose the latter. "We took the time to format a House of Quality chart on our CAD/CAM system," explains Peter J. Soltis, Senior Technical Specialist, Product Engineering, at Kelsey-Hayes. "It took a while to develop that chart, but it helped with all subsequent charts. We can now reduce our preparation time substantially. By using the CAD/CAM system, we can vary the size of the charts depending on the scope of the QFD study."

Implementation Issues

A number of challenges await QFD champions eager to introduce the process to their companies: information overload; time, patience, and discipline issues; QFD's Japanese heritage; proprietary information. In addition, QFD isn't the first product-improvement program American industry has been introduced to; a "prove it to me" attitude often accompanies the implementation of such programs.

Finding the time to complete a QFD case study may prove challenging. QFD may be perceived as an

Management Support Essential

Top management plays a key role in Japanese new-product development. By providing a broad strategic direction for the company, top management helps define the product-development process. This broad strategic direction is the result of constant monitoring of the external environment—identifying competitive threats and market opportunities—and evaluation of company strengths and weaknesses.

Identifying competitive threats and market opportunities and evaluating company strengths and weaknesses are two of the things that QFD does best. To make QFD work, however, American upper management needs to do two of the things it does best:

- Make a commitment to an innovative and rewarding activity.
- Delegate authority to the individuals best suited to make that activity happen.

QFD does require a definite time commitment—a commitment that spans the product-development cycle. By providing your QFD project team with the time to do QFD right, you'll be setting the stage for a successful application.

Managing for success in QFD also entails asking the right questions. What are the right questions? They include the following:

- How was the voice of the customer determined?
- How were the design requirements determined?

(The usual in-house standards should be challenged.)
- How do we compare to our competition?
- What opportunities can we identify to gain a competitive edge?
- What further information do we need? How can we get it?
- What trade-off decisions need to be made?
- What can I do to help?

There are a number of things you can do to help right off the bat—one of which is to ensure that QFD is being performed in an environment conducive to its success. QFD is at its best in a progressive environment that fosters creative endeavors and information-sharing. Although QFD will most likely be directed by a representative of design engineering, it will involve all product-oriented arms of the company.

Management should also push for progress with QFD. But don't push too hard. QFD is essentially a learn-by-doing experience. With the proper encouragement, team members will push the limits of their own learning curve.

Management should provide QFD project team members—or, at the very least, the team leader—with professional instruction in QFD. This instruction will enhance QFD awareness and facilitation, as well as incite further interest in the process. With a QFD champion in the ranks and on the management team, QFD can help your company improve its competitive ranking.

added workload instead of a better way of doing things. It may get lost in the everyday shuffle; it may be perceived as just too time-consuming. Hence, people have a tendency to want to get on with QFD too fast—to try to determine the design requirements before the customer requirements, for example.

It's also important that QFD be integrated into everyday business operations. Otherwise, it will just be an added task. In some cases, QFD may have to be modified in order to make it fit.

QFD requires patience—from both project-team members and upper management. It won't yield a quick return; rather, benefits that are lasting in nature. "Will the American engineer and the American manager have the patience to do QFD, or will the pressures of the everyday job win out?" asks GM's Schaefer. "Up to this point, there's been a great deal of interest and curiosity. But when that wears off will we take the time to fill out the matrices? I'd like to think that we'll have the perseverence to do the job properly."

As Schaefer indicated, QFD requires discipline: It brings discipline to an organization, but it also asks for discipline in return. It requires that people work together and pay strict attention to detail—which isn't always easy.

"Another challenge is promoting the method without relying on success stories," says Michael E. Chupa, Vice President of Marketing, ITT Hancock, Jackson, Michigan. "A company usually can't afford to divulge the results of a QFD case study to its competitors."

Keeping the Momentum

Challenges notwithstanding, QFD case studies are being completed at an accelerating rate across the U.S.—proof that American industry is embracing QFD. Although much of the information contained within these case studies is proprietary, questions and answers regarding QFD's mechanics, benefits, and troublesome aspects must be circulated. Whenever possible, case studies should be shared with others. Public seminars, workshops, and conferences will do much to further this cause, as will in-house seminars and symposia. A QFD user's group would also be extremely beneficial.

Companies faced with burgeoning work loads are going to have to work to keep QFD going strong. In such situations, upper-management support is even more of a prerequisite to success. Management astute enough to recognize the value of QFD should ensure that its support staffs receive the training and hands-on experience necessary to make QFD happen. Management that comes on strong for QFD—with no ifs, ands, or buts—will see the greatest rewards. Management that sees no need or use for QFD should look again—within their organizations and toward the 1990s.

What else should you know about implementing QFD? Ten simple words: Find reasons to succeed with QFD, not excuses for failure.

Tips from QFD Pioneers

"If a company's healthy and getting new business, the best way to get started is by asking how QFD fits into the organizational scheme of things. The first exercise will be a real learning experience, but you won't be disappointed with the results."
  —Michael E. Chupa, Vice President of Marketing, ITT Hancock, Jackson, Michigan

"What QFD will help us overcome— departmentalization—is also one of the barriers that precludes its wide-scale implementation. The first step is to organize a multifunctional team. All functions must be represented."
  —Dr. Don Clausing, Bernard Gordon Adjunct Professor of Engineering Innovation and Practice, Massachusetts Institute of Technology, Cambridge, Massachusetts

"We used a two-part strategy to get QFD started: awareness sessions and facilitation case studies. Each awareness session consisted of a one-hour pitch—20 minutes of prepared presentation and 40 minutes of questions and answers. We approached people at all levels—top executives, middle management, and line engineers."
  —Robert J. Dika, Specialist, Engineering Quality Assurance, Chrysler Corp., Highland Park, Michigan

"You have to be patient—it's going to take time. You can't expect to implement QFD across the board all at once. That's unrealistic—you just won't have the people or the time to do that. Be selective in picking your QFD application and then take it step by step."
  —James T. Gipprich, Director, Market Development, Kelsey-Hayes Co., Romulus, Michigan

"Our conclusion is that you need short-term education of the technique followed by hands-on experience implementing it. You also need access to someone who can review what you've done and help correct and redirect your efforts. Your first QFD project will then be a meaningful exercise."

   —Calvin W. Gray, Group Vice President, Sales
   and International Operations, Sheller-Globe,
   Detroit, Michigan

"Get an example of how QFD's being used so you have a role model in your company and then expand from there. Americans like to see things in actual practice—testimonies that say it's better than what we've been doing. We need good examples in the public domain."

   —Walton M. Hancock, Associate Dean, Center
   for Research on Integrated Manufacturing, College
   of Engineering, University of Michigan, Ann Arbor,
   Michigan

"QFD is like driving a car—you can't learn all about it in a classroom. You have to get behind the wheel and actually engage the clutch. You also have to be flexible in your approach; you have to develop the charts to meet your needs."

   —Norman E. Morrell, Corporate Manager,
   Quality-Product Reliability, The Budd Co., Troy,
   Michigan

"It's important to have a team leader, as well as an outside resource person. The former needs to be a high-potential person who's very credible in the organization and open-minded enough to see different points of view. The latter should be a knowledgeable facilita-

(Continued on the next page)

(continued)

tor who keeps things moving without directing the project and has no direct interest in the particular project."
> —George R. Perry, Vice President, Quality and Reliability, Allied-Signal, Inc., Automotive Sector World Headquarters, Southfield, Michigan

"To quote Mr. Fukuhara, you've got to 'pick up the pencil.' You can talk and talk and talk about it, but until you actually start defining the voice of the customer and creating a chart, it's all talk. You don't have to do things perfectly—there's a lot of benefit from just making an attempt."
> —Robert H. Schaefer, Reliability Engineering Director, Product Assurance and Validation, Chevrolet-Pontiac-Canada Group, General Motors Corp., Warren, Michigan

"Putting the information down and keeping it up to date is a fairly labor-intensive procedure that someone needs to be responsible for. That someone may vary among companies depending on how they are organized."
> —Raymond P. Smock, Manager, Advanced Quality Concepts Development, Product Assurance, Ford North American Automotive Operations, Dearborn, Michigan

"The mechanics of QFD can be learned from a seminar. The actual information that you get from the marketplace, however, really makes QFD meaningful. Formulating a questionnaire, sending it off, analyzing the results—these are very important aspects of QFD."
> —Peter J. Soltis, Senior Technical Specialist, Product Engineering, Kelsey-Hayes Co., Romulus, Michigan

APPENDIX
Taguchi Methods

Quality Function Deployment (QFD) is often used in conjunction with Taguchi Methods in Japan. The two processes are complementary in nature. QFD identifies the relationships between inputs ("how" items) and outputs ("what" items), as well as conflicting inputs that must be balanced. Many questions are raised during the QFD process, such as "What is the nature of the relationships?" and "What is the best value for the 'how much' items?" Taguchi Methods define the nature of those relationships and optimize conflicting inputs (see **Figure A-1**). As described below, Taguchi Methods desensitize the outputs of uncontrollable inputs, which reduces performance variation. This reduction in variability results in reduced cost and improved performance and quality.

Dr. Genichi Taguchi developed Taguchi Methods—combined engineering and statistical methods

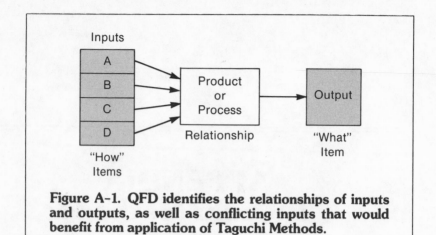

Figure A-1. QFD identifies the relationships of inputs and outputs, as well as conflicting inputs that would benefit from application of Taguchi Methods.

that achieve rapid improvements in cost and quality by optimizing product design and manufacturing processes. Taguchi Methods are both a philosophy and a collection of tools used to carry forth that philosophy (see **Figure A–2**).

Taguchi's philosophy can be summed up by the following statements:

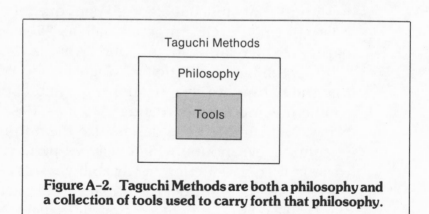

Figure A-2. Taguchi Methods are both a philosophy and a collection of tools used to carry forth that philosophy.

1. We cannot reduce cost without affecting quality.
2. We can improve quality without increasing cost.
3. We can reduce cost by improving quality.
4. We can reduce cost by reducing variation. When we do so, performance and quality will automatically improve.

Taguchi disagrees with the "conformance to specification limits" approach to quality: The difference between a product barely within specification limits (1, **Figure A-3**) and a product barely out of specification limits (2, **Figure A-3**) is small, yet one is considered "good" and the other "bad." Rather, Taguchi Methods strive for minimal variation around target values without adding cost.

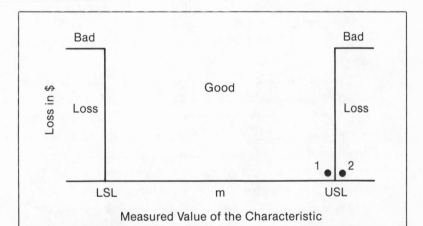

Measured Value of the Characteristic

Figure A-3. The difference between a product barely within specification limits (1) and a product barely out of specification limits (2) is small, yet one is considered "good" and the other "bad." According to Taguchi, minimal variation around the target value (m) results in reduced costs and consumer loss.

Key Taguchi Terms

Confirmation experiment: An experiment run under the conditions defined as optimum by a previous experiment. It is intended to verify the experimental predictions.

Factor: A parameter or variable that may impact product or process performance.

Linear graph: A graphical representation of the assignment of factors to specific columns of an orthogonal array. Each linear graph is associated with one orthogonal array. However, a given orthogonal array can have several linear graphs.

Noise: Any uncontrollable factor that causes product quality to vary. There are three kinds of noise: 1. "external," or noise due to external causes (i.e. temperature, humidity, operator, vibration, etc.), 2. "internal," or noise due to internal causes (i.e., wear, deterioration, etc.); and 3. "product-to-product," or noise due to part-to-part variation.

Orthogonal array: A matrix of numbers arranged in rows and columns. Each row represents the state of the factors in a given experiment. Each column represents a specific factor or condition that can be changed from test run to test run. The array is called orthogonal because the effects of the various factors in the experimental results can be separated from each other.

Parameter design: The second of three design stages. During parameter design, nominal values of critical dimensions and characteristics are established to optimize performance at low cost.

Quality characteristic: A characteristic of a product or process that defines the product/process quality; a measure of the degree of conformance to some known standard.

Quality Loss Function (QLF): A parabolic approximation of the quality loss that occurs when a quality characteristic deviates from its target value. The QLF is expressed in monetary units.

Robustness: The condition of a product or process design that indicates that it functions with limited variability despite diverse and changing environmental conditions, wear, or component-to-component variation. A product or process is robust when it has limited or reduced functional variation in the presence of noise.

Signal-to-Noise (S/N) Ratio: A quantity characterizing quality that originated in the communications field. When applied to design of experiments, the S/N Ratio is used to evaluate test equipment quality and project field-quality performance from experimental data. The S/N Ratio is a measure that indicates how well variability has been minimized—the larger the ratio, the more robust the product is against noise.

System design: The first of three design stages. During system design, scientific and engineering knowledge is applied to produce a functional prototype design. This prototype is used to define the initial settings of product/process design characteristics.

Tolerance design: The third of three design stages. Tolerance design is applied only if the design isn't acceptable at its optimum level following parameter design. During tolerance design, more costly materials or processes with tighter tolerances are considered.

Taguchi defines quality as the characteristic that avoids "loss to society" from the time a product is shipped. When a product fails to function as expected, it imparts a loss to the customer. The customer may experience this loss on a small and/or large scale: e.g., as the costs associated with repair or replacement of a product or as an environmental hazard created by a product.

When a product is over-designed, there is a loss to the company. The product may even be inferior, because it may be heavier, less efficient, or larger than necessary.

All loss is eventually experienced by the company through warranty costs, customer complaints, litigation, and eventual loss of reputation and market share.

According to Taguchi, quality is best when product characteristics are at target values (see **Figure A-4**). As product characteristics deviate from target values, quality decreases and consumer dissatisfaction and loss increase.

The curve shown in **Figure A-4** is known as the Quality Loss Function (QLF). The QLF is an enhanced cost-control system designed to quantitatively evaluate quality: It assesses quality loss due to deviation of a quality characteristic from its target value and then expresses this loss in monetary units.

The QLF quantifies annual cost savings as quality characteristics improve toward target values—even when within specification limits. It is an excellent tool for evaluating quality at the earliest stage of product/process development.

Thus, reducing sensitivity to variation is a main thrust of Taguchi Methods. Sensitivity to variation is reduced by adjusting factors that can be controlled in a way that minimizes the effects of factors that can't be controlled (see **Figure A-5**). This results in what Taguchi calls a "robust" design. Factors that can be controlled are called control factors; factors that are

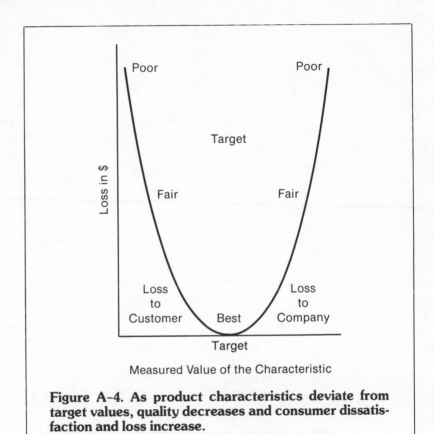

Figure A-4. As product characteristics deviate from target values, quality decreases and consumer dissatisfaction and loss increase.

difficult, impossible, or expensive to control are called noise factors.

Taguchi has identified three types of noise factors: 1. "external" (i.e., temperature, humidity, operator, vibration, etc.), 2. "internal" (i.e., wear, deterioration, etc.), and 3. "product-to-product" (i.e., due to part-to-part variation). Noise factors generally cause product characteristics to deviate from target values, which causes variation and quality loss.

Consider the following nontechnical analogy. We have a number of choices when it comes to the kind of

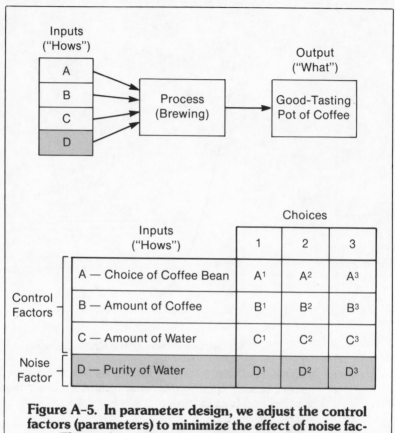

Figure A–5. In parameter design, we adjust the control factors (parameters) to minimize the effect of noise factors. The goal is to find the combination of factors that gives the most stable and reliable performance at the lowest cost.

coffee bean, amount of coffee, and amount of water used to make a pot of coffee. These can be thought of as control factors. Unless we purchase bottled water, or invest in a purification system, however, the purity of the water used to make the pot of coffee is harder to control. Hence, purity of water can be thought of as a noise factor. In parameter design, we adjust the control factors to minimize the effect of the noise factors.

In our nontechnical example, this means finding a cost-effective combination of coffee bean, amount of coffee, and amount of water that tastes best with a variety of water types. The end goal is to make a good-tasting pot of coffee at a low cost.

Control factors that minimize the effects of noise factors (and hence reduce variation) are selected during parameter design, which follows system design (see **Figure A–6**).

The goal of parameter design is to find the combination of materials, processes, and specifications that gives the most stable and reliable performance at the lowest cost through experimentation.

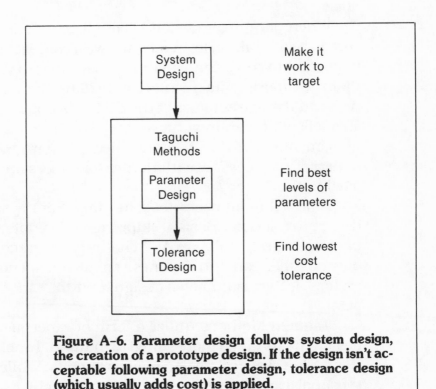

Figure A-6. Parameter design follows system design, the creation of a prototype design. If the design isn't acceptable following parameter design, tolerance design (which usually adds cost) is applied.

This is accomplished by maximizing a measure called the Signal-to-Noise Ratio (S/N Ratio). The S/N Ratio, which originated in the communications field (the signal representing the desired output; the noise, whatever gets in the signal's way), is an objective, statistical measure of performance and the effect of noise factors on performance.

The S/N Ratio measures the *stability* of a quality characteristic's performance. The QLF is then used to evaluate the effect of that stability in monetary units; high performance (a large S/N Ratio) implies low loss (which will be measured by the QLF). The larger the ratio, the more robust the product will be against noise.

When parameter design is complete, the design should be at peak performance at lowest cost. It is very important to run a confirmation experiment to verify that the experimental results can hold up in production and the marketplace. If the design is not acceptable following parameter design, tolerance design is implemented. During tolerance design, more costly materials or processes with tighter tolerances are applied to the design.

American engineers tend to jump from system design to tolerance design, skipping or downplaying parameter design. **Figure A–7** illustrates the amount of time American and Japanese engineers spend on system design, parameter design, and tolerance design.

Taguchi Methods utilize a form of experimental design that is much more suited to industrial applications than classical design of experiments. While orthogonal arrays were not invented by Taguchi, he did

	U.S.	Japan
System Design	70%	40%
Parameter Design	2%	40%
Tolerance Design	28%	20%

Figure A-7. Japanese engineers typically spend equal time on system design and parameter design, whereas U.S. engineers spend the greatest percentage of their time on system design, followed by tolerance design, literally skipping parameter design.

invent linear graphs, which make orthogonal arrays easier to use. Taguchi uses linear graphs with orthogonal arrays to assign different numbers of test settings to factors—the arrays then focus on an average effect that occurs as other conditions change.

Orthogonal arrays have a pair-wise balancing property: The level for each factor occurs the same number of times as levels for all other factors (see **Figure A-8**). This minimizes the number of required experimental runs.

Taguchi Methods are used for both off-line quality control (product- and process-design optimization) and on-line quality control (monitoring of ongoing production processes) in Japan (see **Figure A-9**).

Taguchi has received four Deming Prizes for his work, as well as the Willard F. Rockwell Medal for Excellence in Technology—which recognizes the generation, transfer, and application of technology for the betterment of mankind—from the International Technology Institute.

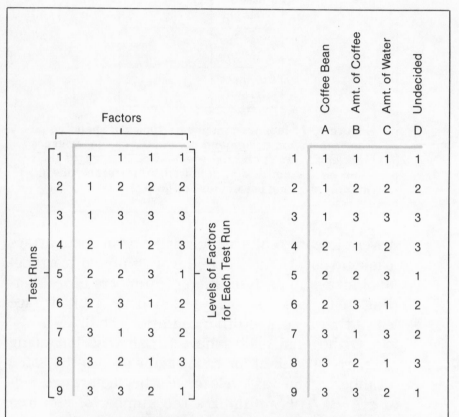

Figure A-8. This orthogonal array, the L_9, features nine test runs with four different factors, each of which is run at three different settings. Each factor is exposed to each setting an equal number of times, which ensures reproducibility of results. Control factors for the pot-of-coffee example are shown at right (the noise factor would be placed in an adjacent outer array).

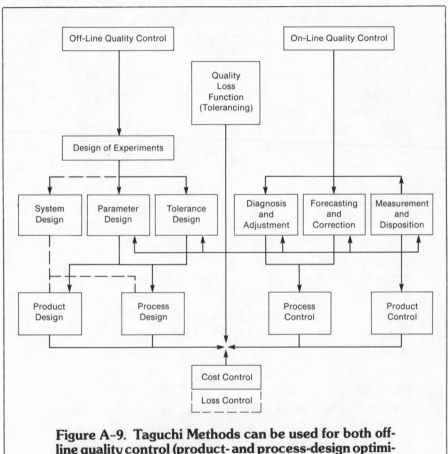

Figure A-9. Taguchi Methods can be used for both off-line quality control (product- and process-design optimization) and on-line quality control (monitoring of ongoing production processes). (Courtesy Dr. W. H. Moore, Ford Motor Co., 1986).

Taguchi Methods Earn U.S. Following

American executives and engineers that support and practice Taguchi Methods are beginning to understand Dr. Genichi Taguchi's premise that quality can be improved without increasing cost.

Many American companies are implementing Taguchi Methods. Because they contain proprietary information, the results of these applications cannot always be made public. Thus, it is difficult to judge just how many applications of Taguchi Methods have been completed in the United States. It is safe to say that well over 5,000 Taguchi Methods case studies are now completed annually in the U.S. (However, the number of Taguchi Methods case studies prepared annually in Japan is estimated to be 20 times this number.)

Dr. Taguchi's methodology was first introduced to the U.S. in the early 1980s. The American Taguchi Methods case studies presented at the First Symposium on Taguchi Methods, hosted by the American Supplier Institute (ASI), Inc., in 1983, were all automotive-related. Now, however, companies in a number of other industries are also using Taguchi Methods.

Case-study preparation and presentation and the resulting technical interaction are important ingredients of Taguchi's Quality Engineering philosophy. ASI's annual Taguchi Methods symposium is a primary avenue for case-study presentation. In addition, a number of companies that have embraced Taguchi Methods are now hosting their own internal symposiums.

In a paper prepared in early 1987, Lawrence P. Sullivan, Chairman and CEO of ASI, shared Taguchi Methods results from three American converts, one large, one medium, and one small in size:

- ITT has trained 1,200 engineers in Taguchi Methods and completed 2,000 case studies, resulting in cost savings of $35,000,000.
- Sheller-Globe has trained 120 engineers in Taguchi Methods, completed 225 case studies, and achieved cost savings of $10,000,000.
- Flex Technologies has trained 12 engineers in Taguchi Methods, completed 75 case studies, and recorded $1,400,000 in cost savings.

American companies can benefit from using Taguchi Methods for both off-line quality control (product- and process-design optimization) and on-line quality control (monitoring of ongoing production processes). The majority of Taguchi Methods case studies performed in the U.S. involve off-line quality-control activities. The challenge is to begin using the methodology for on-line quality-control activities as well, and to use Taguchi Methods in conjunction with Quality Function Deployment.

Index

NOTE: The symbol (F) or (T) following a page number indicates that information is presented in a figure or a table, respectively.

119